The
School Library
at Work

The
School Library
at Work

*Acquisition, Organization, Use and Maintenance
of Materials in the School Library*

by

Azile Wofford

ASSOCIATE PROFESSOR, DEPARTMENT OF LIBRARY SCIENCE, UNIVERSITY OF KENTUCKY

New York: The H. W. Wilson Company
1959

To the memory of my sister
Dr. Kate V. Wofford
late Professor and Head
Department of Elementary Education
University of Florida
who along the family ladder of achievement
always pointed the way

FOREWORD

The school librarian is a different type of librarian, because the school library is a different type of library. The school library is so integral a part of the total school program that it is difficult to say where the school stops and the library begins, if indeed a dividing line can be drawn. The school library is usually in the building which houses all its potential users. The librarian must work shoulder to shoulder with classroom teachers in helping pupils make full use of library materials. In fact, the school librarian *is* a teacher operating through the library rather than a classroom.

Training for the school librarian reflects this difference in the increasing requirement that it include courses in education as well as library science and offer experience in student teaching as well as school library practice. The successful school librarian is apt to have had experience as a teacher also. Unlike other librarians, except those in very small libraries of other types, the school librarian is absolutely on his own. The usual pattern is one trained librarian for a school; sometimes there will be only one trained librarian in the school system. Consequently, there is not much opportunity for the school librarian to learn essential routines on the job. Nor would time permit, even if there were someone to ask who could give the answers. In a school library, no one wants anything tomorrow. Each request for help is pegged at "right now," unless it is a left-over from yesterday. As a result, routines must be reduced to a minimum, simplified so that pupil assistants may handle many of them, and be as free as possible from red tape.

All of which explains why this book is being offered to the field of school librarianship. It should be helpful in the training of school librarians, especially when one course must include both administration of the library and technical processes, as is often the case. The librarian on the job will refer to it, we hope, and use it in training pupil assistants or in directing their work.

Where the school library must be supervised temporarily by an untrained person, help in learning techniques and routines may be obtained from this book. It should also help the administrator realize more fully that administering the school library is a full-time job in itself and that the librarian does not have time for additional duties. The book is designed to be practical, rather than scholarly or technical, since practicality is the cornerstone of any school library at work.

ACKNOWLEDGMENTS

I must acknowledge indebtedness to many people who have contributed to *The School Library at Work*. I derived both philosophy and information from twenty-four former instructors in whose classes I was enrolled in the library schools of the University of North Carolina, George Peabody College for Teachers, Columbia University and the University of Chicago. During more than thirty years in library work, I have added greatly to my knowledge of school libraries by reading books and articles available on the subject. Many of my library colleagues at adjacent desks, during my visits to their libraries, in numerous and sundry library meetings, and across miles of banquet tables have generously shared their practical ideas, a number of which have been incorporated into the pages of this book.

I am deeply indebted to four librarians who read the manuscript as it was being written and offered criticism and suggestions. They are: Margaret Roser, Librarian, University School; Ruby Trower, Supervisor of Library Services, Lexington City Schools; and Ruth Wheeler, Librarian, Morton Junior High School—all of Lexington, Kentucky; and Gertrude Coward, Director of Libraries, Charlotte City Schools, Charlotte, North Carolina. Nella Bailey, Supervisor of School Libraries in the State Department of Education of Kentucky, has served also in an advisory capacity and read the manuscript in its entirety.

Dorothy West and John Jamieson of The H. W. Wilson Company have furnished sound editorial advice in the form of comment, correction, and criticism. They have encouraged me through times of discouragement, curbed enthusiasm for getting on more swiftly than the job warranted, and prevented my saying anything for which the Wilson Company could be sued.

I have had continued encouragement from Dean Martin M. White of the College of Arts and Sciences, University of Kentucky, and the Head of the Department of Library Science, Dr. E. J. Humeston, Jr. The latter has also read the manuscript as added insurance against misplaced commas, split infinitives, and dangling participles.

Last, but not least, I am indebted to several typists who, in preparation of the material for publication, have struggled with my handwriting. I am especially indebted to Carolyn Fisher, secretary of the Department of Library Science, who somehow has found time to help prepare the figures and to lend a hand with the Appendix. Printed forms, with a very few exceptions, were furnished through the courtesy of Gaylord Brothers. Baker and Taylor Company kindly supplied an invoice for the books listed on the sample order.

Yet, with all this help, I alone must accept responsibility for the finished product. Whatever its faults, I am hopeful that the book will prove useful in smoothing the way for future school librarians.

AZILE WOFFORD

Lexington, Kentucky
February 1959

CONTENTS

CHAPTER 1

ACQUISITION OF MATERIALS

Introduction

The acquisition of materials for any school library is so closely tied up with book selection and financial support that it is almost impossible to discuss acquisition without including some discussion of the other two. Because the subject of book selection for school libraries is such a broad one and the materials involved so extensive, only a brief discussion is here included, emphasizing primarily the routines of selection. This chapter merely introduces the subject of financial support which is more fully discussed in Chapter 6, School Library Finances.

Support of the School Library

Since the school library is now considered an integral part of any school program, planned in line with and essential to its educational objectives, support of the school library should be a regular part of the school's annual appropriation. Despite definite standards set by departments of education in the various states, by regional accrediting associations, and by the American Library Association, all too many school libraries are still attempting to carry on library service without adequate funds and, in some cases, without any specified appropriation. Standards for appropriations for school library service are usually based on enrollment of the school or, more recently, on the number of pupils in average daily attendance, and vary from state to state or region to region. The present national standards [1] for school libraries suggest $1.50 per pupil but future revision must surely take into consideration increased costs of library materials. In school li-

[1] American Library Association. *School Libraries for Today and Tomorrow* (Chicago: The Association, 1945)

braries where the appropriation of $1.50 per pupil has already been attained, librarians testify to the fact that it is not sufficient for adequate library service.

Responsibility for the support of the school library rests with the administration and the school board. Vested in these authorities is the obligation to see that the library appropriation meets current standards and is sufficient to insure adequate service to both pupils and teachers. A wise librarian will insist that a regular appropriation for the library be included in the annual school budget, even though it must at first be small, with plans to work toward standards set by authorities in the field as being adequate for the support of school library services. Parent-Teacher Associations and other organizations have often been interested in, and generous with contributions to, local school libraries, especially on the elementary level. And many school librarians have experienced the necessity of sponsoring money-raising programs or directing campaigns for contributions to the library. All such funds, however, should supplement, rather than support, the school library. It cannot be emphasized too strongly that every school library must have a definite, regular appropriation from school funds.

As early in the school year as possible, the librarian should be informed of the appropriation for the library. Suggestions for planning the budget will be considered in Chapter 6. At this point it is sufficient to state that the acquisition of materials is necessarily dependent on the assurance of money with which to purchase them. Because it does not always work out that way, it is urged that any money appropriated for the school library should be made available to it. By the same token, the school librarian is vested with the responsibility of making sure that all money available is actually spent, and wisely spent. Evidence of the latter is often necessary for continued support of the school library. Wise use of available funds is also a strong point when the librarian needs to ask for an increased appropriation for the school library in order to expand services.

Selection of Books

Selection of books for the school library is a continuous process. The librarian is constantly checking lists of books in current book selection aids or noting older titles in standard book selection aids. Teachers and administrators also are often attracted to titles in educational periodicals which might be noted for future purchase. Even students, especially student assistants or good readers, will bring clippings, either reviewing or mentioning books which have appeal for them. This suggests that book selection for the school library is also a cooperative process with librarian, teachers, administrators and pupils all having a part. No one person alone is equal to the task of choosing materials for all levels of reading ability, maturity and interests. The school librarian who attempts such a task will find that the library tends to become the library of the librarian rather than of the school. The librarian knows, or should know, a great deal about library materials, but it is the teacher who knows, or should know, what materials will be most useful in the classroom. The two working together will assure a more adequate, workable collection of books and other materials.

Book Selection Aids

Until the school librarian has gained experience and has established values which will aid in book selection, it is advisable to make the bulk of selection from standard lists. Paramount in importance are the *Standard Catalog for High School Libraries* [2] for all libraries serving high school pupils and the *Children's Catalog* [3] for elementary school libraries. Because of overlapping at the junior high school level, it is almost always necessary to have both these catalogs for junior high school libraries. Many of the titles in the *Children's Catalog* are also included in the *Standard Catalog for High School Libraries*. These book selection aids, with their regular supplements, represent the best in books and

[2] *Standard Catalog for High School Libraries*, 7th ed. (New York: H. W. Wilson Company, 1957)

[3] *Children's Catalog*, 9th ed. (New York: H. W. Wilson Company, 1956)

related materials for school libraries. Both are published by the
H. W. Wilson Company on the service basis, which means that
libraries pay for the aids according to their potential use. School
library rates for the *Standard Catalog for High School Libraries*
are based on enrollment, but the *Children's Catalog* is now available to all schools at a flat rate of $8.00. *A Basic Book Collec-
tion for Elementary Grades, A Basic Book Collection for Junior
High Schools* and *A Basic Book Collection for High Schools* are
compiled by a subcommittee of the American Library Association
Editorial Committee with the assistance of consultants from several organizations and are published by the American Library
Association. These compilations are especially helpful in selecting basic materials for school libraries that are being developed
and as a standard in checking a school library collection already
in existence. A full list of book selection aids with bibliographical
data will be found in the Appendix.

For more recent materials, the school librarian will depend on
current book reviewing periodicals, a list of which is also included
in the Appendix. Among these is *The Booklist and Subscription
Books Bulletin,* containing titles chosen by a group of librarians
working with American Library Association book reviewers and
thorough reviews of reference books sold on the subscription basis,
that is, materials obtainable only directly from the publishers or
their agents, and for which subscriptions are often taken before
publication. Titles of any books of reference nature should be
checked in *The Booklist and Subscription Books Bulletin* for recommendation before purchase. The section "Current Reference
Books" in the *Wilson Library Bulletin* is helpful in choosing reference materials not sold on the subscription basis.

Junior Libraries, contained in each mid-monthly issue of the
Library Journal, is helpful for rather extensive coverage of materials for children and young people and for "difference of
opinion" reviews of some books. *Junior Libraries* is paged separately and may be obtained as a separate magazine, and will
probably serve the needs of the average school library. Larger
school libraries will probably prefer *Library Journal,* including
Junior Libraries. Another useful book selection aid for school

libraries is the *Bulletin of the Center for Children's Books* in Chicago which, by the use of a lettered code, indicates whether the book is or is not recommended and gives other helpful information. For selection of books for younger children, the *Horn Book* is as necessary as is the *Saturday Review* for adult books. The *Saturday Review* also includes reviews of books for young readers in one issue each month. Some school librarians feel that both the *Horn Book* and the *Saturday Review* are more helpful in selecting books for young children than books for adolescents.

Consideration File

School librarians will find helpful for elusive items which might be considered for future purchase a consideration or "want" file. This temporary record may be made on 3″ by 5″ cards and should contain all the bibliographical information on the book or pamphlet available at the time the card is made. It should also carry some explanation as to why the book seems desirable. This could be because a teacher mentioned, or requested, it; because it was reviewed in a certain publication; or because the book was examined in another library or recommended by a fellow librarian. Unless a record is made then, precious time is wasted later attempting to recapture information on a vaguely remembered item. For weeding purposes, in case the item is not actually purchased, it is well to stamp the date on which the card was added to the file. As an aid in using the file for selection of materials, it is also helpful to place at the top of the card the subject, department, or area of the budget to which the item would probably be assigned. Thus an accumulation of purchase suggestions will be available when an order is to be placed (Figure 1).

It is well to consult the consideration file each time an order is to be made and, if an order card is made for the title, the corresponding card in the consideration file should be removed and destroyed. Frequent weeding of cards which have been in the file for a reasonable time, e.g., the duration of the school year, without having been ordered will help keep the consideration file

```
┌────────────────────────────────────────────────────────────┐
│                                          March 11, 1957      │
│       SCIENCE                                                │
│                                                              │
│    Fenton, Carroll Lane and Mildred (Adams)                  │
│                                                              │
│       Our changing weather.  Doubleday, 1954.  $2.50         │
│                                                              │
│                                                              │
│       Miss Jones would like for unit on the weather.         │
│                                                              │
│                          or                                  │
│                                                              │
│       Mr. Smith says reviewed favorably in Science           │
│    Monthly.                                                  │
│                                                              │
│                                                              │
└────────────────────────────────────────────────────────────┘
```

FIGURE 1
Card for consideration file

up to date. This is where the date stamped on the card at time of entry in the file proves its usefulness.

Request Slips

Another source for consideration in ordering is a file of request slips submitted by administrators, teachers and pupils. Request slips may be planned to fit school needs and mimeographed in the school. A supply of these slips available at all times should result in increased requests by teachers for books to be purchased. Where a consideration file is not kept, the librarian will find request slips convenient for recording information about a book which seems desirable for the collection. The request slip might well be a duplicate of the order card, though it will be cheaper to use request slips rather than actual order cards for purchase requests, both because order cards are more expensive and because many requests will not be ordered and the cards will thus be wasted. A request slip might follow the sample shown in Figure 2.

Frequent conferences with teachers as to types of materials needed and weaknesses of the present collection will encourage the

Author (surname first)		
Title		
		No. cops.
Publisher	Date	Price
Edition	Series	
Requested by:		

FIGURE 2
Suggested form for request slip

filling out and submitting of request slips. The librarian should
not only build up a good collection of book selection aids in the
school library but also encourage teachers to choose materials
from them. Teachers should be notified as to the time for sending regular orders so that they will know when to request needed
materials. The librarian's role is to coordinate orders, conferring
with teachers when there seems to be unnecessary duplication,
perhaps suggesting other titles than those requested and pointing
out available new editions of desired titles. The school librarian
will also strive to keep some balance between the various types of
materials in the collection so that all interests of pupils and
teachers and the needs of all departments of the school will be
represented. When teachers fail to make requests, the librarian
must assume the major responsibility for selecting materials in
otherwise neglected areas. Other reading matter will be selected
by the librarian also, especially books for recreational reading
not ordinarily requested for curriculum needs.

Requests from students usually arise from calls that cannot be
filled at the circulation desk. Request slips may be filled out there

and left with the pupil assistant. While the librarian may not
order the actual title suggested, requests from pupils help to indicate the types of materials which interest them. No librarian,
however, would fill the school library shelves with books in undesirable series simply because pupils have requested them.

Frequency of Book Orders

The frequency of book orders will depend on the size of the
school, the amount of money appropriated, and the need for frequent replenishing of current materials. Some very small schools
might send no more than two orders during the year. For some
schools it works well to order four times a year, October, January,
March and May. Larger schools may conceivably send a monthly,
or even weekly, order. A minimum of one order in the fall and
another in the spring would make it possible for any school
library to have new books for circulation early in the school year,
yet have some new materials coming between orders since not all
orders can be filled immediately. Any experienced librarian
knows that a few new books on the shelves tend to increase reading even of the older books. A small amount of the book fund
should be kept to purchase books urgently needed to meet special
classroom demands or to take advantage of new materials as they
are published.

Sources from Which Books May Be Ordered

There are several sources from which school libraries may
order materials. Local bookstores are convenient for that occasional title so urgently needed that one cannot wait to place an
order. Local bookstore owners, however, cannot ordinarily afford
to give more than token discounts, if any. Book orders placed
direct with publishers would probably be assured of prompt delivery and publishers are usually generous in allowing discounts to
libraries. However, the sending of separate orders to individual
publishers entails a great deal of clerical work in orders to be
written, bills to be handled, and checks to be drawn and mailed.
There is also the problem of receiving and processing in the li-

brary a few books at various times rather than a fairly large group at one time.

School libraries will find it generally satisfactory to order from a regular book dealer, or jobber. Such a firm has contacts with most publishers and can either secure books not in stock or have them sent directly from publisher to library. One order and one bill will usually take care of a shipment of books. Book jobbers are also prepared to give good discounts to school libraries, sometimes as much as one third off, a great help where budgets are limited and demands numerous.

Reliable jobbers will also offer special services, such as sending lists of remainders or other books at less than the usual price and allowing the privilege of "books on approval." This is a great help, especially for school librarians who very often have little opportunity to examine books before ordering. Even when selection is made entirely from standard lists, some of the material recommended may not prove suitable for a particular school library. The privilege of examination of materials about which the librarian may be doubtful is always appreciated. This privilege is, however, granted chiefly to libraries which place large orders and then only when the librarian has indicated at the time the order was placed that the book was to be sent on approval. Jobbers are prepared to take back any material arriving in the library not in perfect condition. Imperfect material should be returned as soon as the flaw is discovered, rather than after the book has become a part of the collection, though a reliable jobber will still make it good. This is a good reason for examining all material as soon as possible after it is received in the library.

While the majority of orders from a school library may be submitted to a book dealer, some materials must be ordered direct from the agency issuing them. Examples of this type are: materials issued by organizations such as the American Library Association, National Education Association, National Council of Teachers of English and many others; government publications, local, state and national; materials from certain specialized publishers such as the R. R. Bowker Company or the H. W. Wilson Company; and all materials published on the subscription basis.

Usually there is no discount allowed off the list price on such materials.

Selection of a Dealer

Selection of a dealer will depend somewhat on the area in which the school library is located. Two reliable dealers of long standing in the book field are Baker and Taylor Company of Hillside, New Jersey, and A. C. McClurg and Company of Chicago. The American News Company, through its various branches in many cities, does considerable business with school libraries. There are local concerns also which, through prompt attention to orders, good discounts, and a cooperative spirit, have become favorite dealers for school librarians to patronize.

The new school librarian will probably be guided somewhat by the dealer whom the school library has previously patronized or follow the advice of other librarians in the area. Discussion of book dealers with their merits and weaknesses is a favorite topic even among experienced librarians. It would be well for the inexperienced school librarian to correspond with one or more jobbers, finding out about deliveries, discounts, and special services before deciding to place an order. A visit to the book dealer is a very helpful practice and will give opportunity to talk over matters of mutual interest and benefit to both book dealer and librarian. Correspondence should be entered into to establish routines which will facilitate the process of ordering. It often pays to follow suggestions of the book dealer as to the form desired for the order, rather than insisting on a pattern established by the library. Getting books promptly and in good condition is the important factor in book ordering.

Relation with Agents

Any school librarian eventually faces the problem of what to do about publishers' representatives and other agents who somehow choose the busiest time to visit the school library. To combat this, many schools have the regulation that no salesman may visit classrooms or the library during hours of the school day. Regard-

less of when the librarian talks with agents, a word of warning
seems pertinent against being pressured into buying material from
publishers' representatives without investigating thoroughly its
authenticity and value to the school library. Standard lists should
be checked for inclusion of the material and, in the case of sets of
books, to ascertain whether they are recommended by the Subscription Books Committee. Evaluations are included in semi-
monthly issues of *The Booklist and Subscription Books Bulletin*
published by the American Library Association, as stated earlier.
For reference books not sold on the subscription basis, the section
in each monthly issue of the *Wilson Library Bulletin* called "Current Reference Books" should be consulted. It is well also to have
an understanding with administrators that they should never purchase materials until the librarian has been consulted and given
time to check standard book selection aids. A representative from
reliable firms will understand the reasons for this procedure and
will welcome investigation of the material which he offers. One
who tries to pressure the school librarian into buying materials
without investigation is most probably offering a product that is
not recommended.

Another type of book salesman who sometimes visits school
libraries is a free-lance dealer who offers a collection of books
for sale to schools. It is recommended that the librarian avoid
purchase of books in this way, largely because there is not time
to consult book selection aids or to consider the value of the materials to the present library collection. Such a dealer is apt to
handle an inferior type of book purchased from remainder lists
or from publishers of books rejected by the better known publishers. Furthermore, dealers of this type can hardly afford to give
the liberal discounts needed by school libraries.

Another practice against which the inexperienced school librarian might be warned is that of placing extensive orders with
publishers' or dealers' representatives at conventions. Exhibits of
materials offer a splendid opportunity for examination, but conventions where materials are on exhibit do not afford sufficient
leisure for consideration. Orders submitted under such conditions

will also confuse the order records kept in the library, since they are outside regular procedure.

Book Clubs

It is possible to purchase books for school library use through a variety of book clubs. *Junior Libraries* in each monthly issue lists the current selection of the following book clubs: Arrow Book Club, Catholic Children's Book Club, Junior Literary Guild, Parents' Magazine Book Club, Teen-Age Book Club, Weekly Reader Children's Book Club, Young People's Division of the Literary Guild.

The Junior Literary Guild, the oldest of the book clubs for young readers and probably the most widely used, is taken as an example of how a book club operates. The Junior Literary Guild is a division of Doubleday and Company, publishers in Garden City, New York. The club books are chosen from publishers' manuscripts by the editor, Helen Ferris, and a board of outstanding consultants. One book a month is selected for each of the following age groups: 5-6, 7-8, and 9-11 years. For the upper group, ages 12-16 years, one selection is made for girls and another for boys.

Books may be ordered from the club by either of two methods. The automatic shipment subscription is available at a yearly cost of $19.20 for the twelve books in each age group; each title is mailed to the subscribing library as it is selected by the editors. On a non-automatic shipment subscription basis, the library may purchase a minimum of six books from each age group within the year, with not more than two copies of any one title. No books are shipped without an order from the library. The price under this method is $19.80 for twelve books or $1.65 per book. Since the list price of each Junior Literary Guild selection is $2.00 or more, and all books are in reinforced bindings, there is considerable saving in the book club plan. There is the further advantage of having an assortment of new books arriving all during the school year to pique the interest of the library's users. Before school libraries depend too heavily on securing books through book clubs, however, they should know what the club has to offer and how prices compare with those of books obtained through regular trade channels. Generally speaking, the final selection should be that of the school librarian and the teachers who best understand the needs of the individual library and which books more nearly meet these needs. No book should be ordered from a book club, any more than from other sources, unless it is actually needed in the library.

Preliminary Steps in Ordering

Procedure for placing orders will depend in part on the general regulations of the school system. The librarian should check with the administrator and follow accepted practice, unless it seems to conflict with necessary library techniques. When any changes seem advisable, usually a conference with the administrator will result in a routine satisfactory to both the librarian and business office. The library should have on file a copy of any orders charged against the library budget and keep a simple financial record, apart from the files of the office where bills are actually paid, that will enable anyone who needs to know to ascertain how much has been spent and how much of the appropriation still remains. This will be discussed more fully in Chapter 6.

When decision has been made as to which titles are to be ordered, request slips for these titles should be checked with the card catalog to avoid unnecessary duplication, and also against the file of "books on order" to avoid reordering. If it turns out that the book is on order or already available in the collection, the person making the request should be consulted to determine whether the available copy will be sufficient or if another is actually needed. Generally speaking, no school library collection should contain many duplicates of the same titles. On the other hand, some material is in such great demand that additional copies are needed to meet classroom needs. The policy governing duplication should lie sensibly between the one extreme of the librarian who insists on only one copy of any book and the other extreme of the teacher who would like a copy for each student in the classroom. Here again close cooperation is needed between teachers and librarian. It is well for the library to have a limit beyond which duplication of titles cannot be allowed out of the library appropriation, other funds presumably being available for further added copies.

After a check of the card catalog and the file of books on order, the request slips should be searched in book selection aids for complete and correct bibliographical data, each item being filled in or revised on the slip. For titles not included in book selection aids, the librarian may wish to check the slips against the *Cumulative Book Index,* "a world list of books in the English language." [4] Since most school libraries are not subscribers to this bibliographical service, the *Cumulative Book Index* files of a neighboring public or college library may be used for checking data. Book dealers are generally cooperative in filling orders even when bibliographical details are incomplete. The school librarian is wise, however, to cite data as fully as possible.

At the time that slips are being checked, the availability of Wilson printed catalog cards, indicated by (W) in the *CBI,* should be noted, if this has not already been done. Or, if Library of Congress printed catalog cards are to be used, the L.C. number (for example, 58-2635) should be taken down for later ordering of cards. Information regarding printed catalog cards is available in the *CBI,* the *Standard Catalog for High School Libraries,* and many other book selection aids. *Children's Catalog* designates only Wilson cards, since Library of Congress cards would usually not be used in a library for readers at the elementary level. If a notation on the availability of printed catalog cards is included on the order card for each book it will not need to be looked up later when cards are to be ordered. School librarians are strongly advised to use printed cards whenever available, rather than type-written cards.

Making Order Cards

An order card should now be prepared for each title, with information from the request slips. Since the order card must be

---

[4] Subscriptions to the *Cumulative Book Index* (New York: H. W. Wilson Company) are sold on the service basis of charge.

retained for some time, it should be typed, if possible, or done neatly in ink. Order cards are available from library supply houses and should be selected for suitability to the school library. The sample included here shows how the card will look when the book is ordered (Figure 3).

Class No.	Author (surname first)
	Wilder, Laura (Ingalls)
Accession No.	Title
	By the shores of Silver Lake.
No. of copies ordered	
1	
Date ordered	Volumes
10/25/57	
Of	Publisher Edition or series
B & T	**Harper** **Newly illus. uniform ed.**
Date received	Illustrator Year of publication
	Garth Williams **1953**
Date of bill	Price No. of copies desired
	2.75 **1**
Cost per copy	Department for which recommended
	Elementary social studies
L. C. card No.	Teacher making request
(W)	**Miss Manning**
	Reason for request
	Unit on pioneer days
GAYLORD 101-S	PRINTED IN U.S.A

FIGURE 3
Order card when book is ordered

The author's name should be given in full and the title should be followed by a subtitle, if one is given, and by "ed. by," or "tr. by" if there is an editor or translator for the book. The illustrator's name should be included in the space for that *if* a particular illustrator is desired as in the case of classics and other older books illustrated by various illustrators. It is important that the edition, if other than the first, be indicated on the order card and the series added in parentheses, if the book belongs to a series. The publisher and year of publication or the copyright date, written "c1958," should be given and, where a date is not found, as may be the case for classics and other older books, "n.d." should be used to indicate no date. The price on the order card is that found listed in book selection aids. It is wise to indicate the number of copies desired, even when ordering only one, so that anybody handling order records will understand. The person typing orders from the order cards should be instructed to copy exactly what is on the order card.

Writing the Book Order

After the order cards are prepared, they should be arranged in the sequence to be used in writing the order. In a short order, this should be alphabetically by the author's name. For a longer order, book dealers may prefer that the titles be arranged in groups alphabetically by publisher, and within the groups alphabetically by author. As suggested previously, it is advisable for the librarian to consult the book jobber as to the form of order he prefers.

A letter on school stationery addressed to the book jobber and signed by the librarian should include the following information:

1. How the books are to be shipped.
2. To whom the shipment should be addressed.
3. How many copies of the bill will be needed. It is wise to ask that one copy be sent with the books as an invoice.
4. How the discount is to be indicated. It simplifies records if the discount is deducted from each item rather than from the total, so that the exact cost of each book may be charged to the proper fund.
5. A request for report on items that cannot be supplied or will be delayed in shipment.

Unless the order is very short, the letter should be on a separate sheet attached to the order. Otherwise, the letter may be followed on the same page by the order. To prevent delay in receiving any order, correspondence with the dealer about *anything* other than the present order should not be entered into in the letter accompanying the order. In both the letter and the order, there should be wide margins and on the order itself space should be left between items for notations made at the book jobber's by those who handle the order. The sample order (Figure 4) illustrates bibliographical form and types of entry.

A. B. C. School for Boys

Davenport, Kentucky

Order no.   October 25, 1957
 5

No. copies   Price

  1   Adshead, Gladys L. comp.   Inheritance of poetry.
            Houghton, 1948. $4.00

  1   Association for Childhood Education International
            Told under spacious skies. Macmillan, 1952.   3.00

  1   Benns, Frank Lee. Europe since 1914. 8th ed.
            Appleton, 1954.   5.50

  2   Fenton, Carroll Lane and Mildred (Adams) Our
            changing weather. Doubleday, 1954. ea. $2.50 5.00

  1   Harrer, Heinrich. Seven years in Tibet; tr. by
            Richard Graves. Dutton, 1953.   5.00

  1   Hatch, Alden. General Ike; a biography of Dwight
            D. Eisenhower. Rev. and enl. ed. Holt, 1952. 3.00

  2   Kantor, Mackinlay. Gettysburg; illus. by Donald
            McKay. Random House, 1952. (Landmark books)
            ea. $1.50.   3.00

  1   Log-cabin lady. Little, 1922.   1.50

  1   Porter, Jane. Scottish chiefs; ed. by K. D. Wiggin
            and N. A. Smith; illus. by N. C. Wyeth, Scribner,
            1921.   3.50

  1   Previté-Orton, Charles William. Shorter Cambridge
            medieval history. Cambridge, 1952. 2v.   12.50

  1   Wilder, Laura (Ingalls) By the shores of Silver
            Lake; illus. by Garth Williams. Newly illus-
            trated, uniform ed. Harper, 1953.   2.75

  1   Zim, Herbert Spencer and Martin, Alexander Campbell.
            Trees: a guide to familiar American trees. Simon
            & Schuster, 1952. (Golden nature guide)   1.50

FIGURE 4
Sample order

Duplicate copies of the order should be made as required by the school's regulations. There should be at least one copy for the library files and one for the business office. On the copies kept by the school, it is advisable to total the amount of the order as a means of estimating how much is being spent on each order; this total need not be shown on the original order sent to the dealer. A library can usually count on a discount of 20 per cent in estimating.

After the order has been written, the order cards should be filled out on the left with the following information: number of copies ordered, date ordered and name of dealer (Figure 3). An order for printed catalog cards should also be made, using information on the order card, so that there will be no delay when the books arrive. The order cards are then filed alphabetically by author in the "books on order" file to await arrival of the books.

Handling a Book Order from the Dealer

When a package of books arrives from the dealer, it is wise not to unpack it until there is time to check the invoice. Eager hands await the opportunity to handle new books and avid readers covet the privilege of being first to read a new book. Consequently, unless precautions are taken, some of the books may be missing when time is found to work on them.

By request, a copy of the list of books ordered will be included with the package as an invoice. It should include a report on titles that cannot be supplied or will be delayed in shipment. If the dealer reports that the desired book is out of stock and will be sent later, the librarian should wait a reasonable time for the order to be completed before writing to the dealer again. Meanwhile, a metal or plastic signal of a designated color placed on the card for such a book will facilitate later handling in the outstanding order file. However, if the notation on the invoice suggests that the book, now out of stock, be ordered later, the order card should be drawn from the outstanding order file and placed with other cards awaiting the next order. When "o.p." is noted for a desired title, signifying that the book is out of print, the order card for that book should be drawn from the file, marked "o.p." and placed with those for other out-of-print books awaiting an order to a regular dealer in such materials.

As the books are unpacked and checked, they should be arranged in the order of listing on the invoice. The person checking the order should initial the invoice on the left so that questions may later be referred to the proper person. This is a good practice for all procedures in the school library where pupil help is used.

Working from the invoice, the assistant pulls the order card for each book from the outstanding order file and adds to it on the left the date received, date of bill, and cost per copy (Figure 5). The price for each book on the invoice will be that after

Class No.	Author (surname first)	
	Wilder, Laura (Ingalls)	
Accession No.	Title	
	By the shores of Silver Lake.	
No. of copies ordered		
1		
Date ordered	Volumes	
10/25/57		
Of	Publisher	Edition or series
B & T	Harper	Newly illus. uniform ed.
Date received	Illustrator	Year of publication
11/15/57	Garth Williams	1953
Date of bill	Price	No. of copies desired
11/6/57	2.75	1
Cost per copy	Department for which recommended	
2.20	Elementary social studies	
L. C. card No.	Teacher making request	
(W)	Miss Manning	
	Reason for request	
	Unit on pioneer days	
GAYLORD 101-S	PRINTED IN U.S.A	

FIGURE 5
Order card after book has been received

discount has been allowed and is used for all records in the library. At the same time, from the order card there is entered on the invoice the department, or area of instruction, which requested each book and to which it will be charged. Subtotals should then be computed for each department represented. The person entering this information should initial the right side of the invoice.

This preliminary bookkeeping will facilitate matters greatly in making the record of finances as discussed in Chapter 6. The invoice (Figure 6) for the books ordered on the sample order illustrates the procedures described here. The checked invoice should be kept with others until the actual bill for the shipment arrives and, after consulting the invoice, the librarian approves the bill for payment.

Disposition of the Order Card

The order card should be placed in each book to be cataloged, since the card contains the full bibliographical information necessary in preparing the book for the shelves. Once the cataloging has been completed, the order card may be filed in a "books-received" file and kept for the current school year or until the need to consult it further has passed, after which it may be discarded.

In libraries where the librarian has not yet taken a course in cataloging and so should not undertake to catalog the collection, the order card may, by the addition at upper left corner of the call number obtained from the book itself, be used as a temporary shelf-list card until a permanent shelf-list card is made when the book is cataloged. The method of assigning call numbers will be discussed in Chapter 2. It is suggested that the accession number, which will also be explained in Chapter 2, be placed on the back of the order card thus used. Since space on the front is provided for only one accession number, it will not suffice in case of duplicate copies of a book or when there are several volumes in a set. When the permanent shelf-list card is filed, this card is removed and may be discarded.

Ordering Printed Catalog Cards

This section begins with the repeated admonition that no school librarian should type catalog cards for a book if printed cards are available. Earlier in the chapter, the librarian was advised to order printed catalog cards as soon as the book order is sent to the dealer. For that reason a (W) or the L.C. card number was noted on each order card when the availability of printed cards was indicated in book selection aids. Cataloging of books will be delayed if one waits until after the books arrive before ordering cards. It is true this procedure may mean that some printed cards will be on hand for books that have not been delivered, but eventually the library will secure the books, and the cards can be held until that time. In a school library it is important that new books reach the readers as speedily as possible.

Wilson Catalog Cards

Wilson catalog cards are available from the H. W. Wilson Company. Each card contains in addition to the usual bibliographical information, a brief annotation which is useful in identifying the book for the reader. This service is particularly useful in a busy school library where pupils must learn to find things for themselves. Cards may be obtained either with or without printed subject headings and classification numbers at the top of the cards. School libraries using subject headings in red, a desirable feature in catalogs used by young readers, will probably prefer the cards without the subject headings printed in black capitals. Also many school librarians prefer to assign classification numbers themselves to take care of variations in their particular libraries. Wilson cards are sold in sets only, each set containing all cards needed for the complete cataloging of one title. Each set is priced at 10 cents, though 20 cents is charged for the first title in any order. Some money is saved, therefore, by ordering a considerable number of sets of cards in the same order. The minimum billing for a catalog card order is $2.50; cash must accompany orders under that amount.

The coupon plan, designed to eliminate bookkeeping for the librarian, is the simplest plan for ordering Wilson cards. Ten-cent coupons are sold in sheets of 25 for $2.50. Coupons are attached to each order for printed cards, two coupons for the first title in the order and one coupon for each additional title. If the school librarian prefers, sets of cards may be ordered as needed and billed direct at the end of each quarter. This arrangement is

FORM 83 11-55

DUPLICATE INVOICE

Books sent as ordered NOT RETURNABLE without consent

Not responsible for Goods sent out to be packed or sent by mail uninsured. All claims MUST be made immediately upon receipt of goods.

The Baker & Taylor Co.

HILLSIDE, NEW JERSEY

CABLE: BAKTAY

WHOLESALE BOOKSELLERS · B&T · FOUNDED 1828

THIS IS YOUR FILE NUMBER

No. 4000

MARK IT ON YOUR ORDERS

DATE 11/6/57

SOLD TO

A. B. C. SCHOOL FOR BOYS

DAVENPORT,

KENTUCKY

TERMS: NET CASH

PAYABLE IN NEW YORK FUNDS

Your Order No. 5   Dept. No.

✓	1	ADSHEAD	INHERITANCE OF POETRY	4.00	20	3 20	Elem.
✓	1	ASSOC. FOR CHILDHOOD EDUC. INTERN.	TOLD UNDER SPACIOUS SKIES	3.00	20	2 40	Elem.
✓	1	BENNS	EUROPE SINCE 1914	5.50	20	4 40	Hist.
✓✓	2	FENTON	OUR CHANGING WEATHER	2.50	20	4 00	Sci.
✓	1	HARRER	SEVEN YEARS IN TIBET	5.00	20	4 00	Hist.
✓	1	HATCH	GENERAL IKE	3.00	20	2 40	Rec.

	✓✓ 2	KANTOR	GETTYSBURG	1.50	20	2 40	Hist.	
	✓ 1		LOG-CABIN LADY	1.50	20	1 20	Rec.	
	✓ 1	PORTER	SCOTTISH CHIEFS	3.50	20	2 80	Rec.	
	✓ 1	PREVITE-ORTON	SHORTER CAMBRIDGE MEDIEVAL HISTORY	12.50	20	10 00	Hist	
	✓ 1	WILDER	BY THE SHORES OF SILVER LAKE	2.75	20	2 20	Elem.	
D.C	✓ 1	MARTIN & ZIM	TREES	1.50	20	1 20	Elem.	B.T.
			POST. & INS.			75		
		Elem. $9.00					40 95	
		Hist. 20.80						
		Rec. 6.40						
		Sci. 4.00						
		$40.20						

SHORT ITEMS IF ANY ARE ON ORDER WITH PUBLISHERS AND WILL BE SHIPPED PROMPTLY WHEN RECEIVED.

FIGURE 6

Invoice on books ordered

available only to libraries that order at least $10 worth of cards each quarter.

The catalog card order form, filled out for titles of the sample order for which Wilson cards are available, is shown in Figure 7. Information needed, as will be noted, is the author, title, and edition, if other than the first, and is taken from the order cards for books. A monthly checklist of books cataloged is issued free to all libraries ordering Wilson cards. There is also a weekly checklist, available at an annual charge of $2.00, which might be needed by the larger high school libraries. Because of additional time required to fill them, 20 cents per set is charged on orders for cards that are not arranged alphabetically by the author and also on orders containing titles not included in the checklist.

Library of Congress Cards

For some years, school librarians felt that printed cards from the Library of Congress were too complicated and too detailed for practical use in any but very large senior high school libraries. However, since the Library of Congress cards have more recently been simplified and now conform more closely to typed cards and Wilson printed cards, school libraries are beginning to make use of them when Wilson cards are not available. In fact, in many school library card catalogs, Wilson printed cards, Library of Congress cards, and cards typed in the library serve side by side and pupils do not question minor differences.

School librarians wishing to order Library of Congress cards should write to the Card Division, Library of Congress, Washington 25, D.C., requesting instructions for ordering, a subscriber's card, and printed forms for submitting card orders. For more details on the use of printed cards in cataloging, see Chapter 10 of Akers' *Simple Library Cataloging.*[5]

Out-of-Print Books

If a book is known to be out of print at the time an order is being sent, and book selection aids often do indicate this by

[5] Susan Grey Akers. *Simple Library Cataloging.* 4th ed. (Chicago: American Library Association, 1954)

CATALOG CARD ORDER FORM

FOR PROMPT DELIVERY
PLEASE FILL OUT
PERFORATED MAILING FORM

SEND CARDS — (CHECK ONE!)

☐ WITH subject headings and classification numbers at top of cards

☒ WITHOUT

FROM
THE H. W. WILSON CO.
980 University Avenue
New York 52, N. Y.

(PLEASE PRINT)

TO

LIBRARIAN Mary Smith, Librarian

A.B.C. School for Boys

Davenport, Kentucky

....

▷ IMPORTANT: PRINT YOUR NAME & ADDRESS BELOW — ALSO! ◁

HOW TO ORDER PRINTED CATALOG CARDS. Enclose 1 coupon for each set ordered plus 1 additional coupon for the entire order.
For example: If you order *10 sets send 11 coupons; for 20 sets send 21 coupons.*
List the cards desired in alphabetical order by author and title and consult our checklists when ordering. IT WILL BE NECESSARY TO CHARGE 20c PER SET FOR ALL ORDERS OUT OF ALPHABETICAL ARRANGEMENT OR FOR THOSE ORDERS WHICH CONTAIN TITLES NOT LISTED IN OUR CHECKLISTS. Only those titles listed in The H. W. Wilson Checklists are available.

LIST ALPHABETICALLY — BY AUTHOR PLEASE

Adshead Inheritance of poetry

Benns Europe since 1914

Fenton Our changing weather

Hatch General Ike. Rev. and enl. ed.

Kantor Gettysburg

Previte-Orton Shorter Cambridge medieval history. 2v.

Wilder By the shores of Silver Lake

Zim Trees

ORDERED BY — (PLEASE FILL OUT!)

Mary Smith, Librarian
NAME
A.B.C. School for Boys
ADDRESS
Davenport, Kentucky

NUMBER OF COUPONS ENCLOSED

10

PLEASE USE OTHER SIDE FOR ADDITIONAL ORDERS

4-58—160M(1155)MR

FIGURE 7
Order form for Wilson catalog cards

"o.p.," the title should not be included in an order to a regular book dealer. Instead, order cards for such books should be kept together until an order can be made up and sent to a book jobber dealing in out-of-print books. When a book is reported out of print on the invoice of an order, thus indicating that it cannot be supplied in regular trade, the order card for that title should also be added to the file of order cards for books to be ordered from a dealer in out-of-print books.

Books are declared out of print when book dealers cannot supply copies from stock and copies are no longer available from the publisher. Out-of-print titles often appear among second-hand books or remainders, and dealers often handle all types of hard-to-secure materials. Especially if demand for an out-of-print title is heavy, the price of the book is apt to rise. Consequently, as a safeguard, the school librarian should either have a statement as to the price of a desired out-of-print title before ordering, or state to the dealer a price beyond which the library will not go to secure a copy. Otherwise, the cost of the book may far outweigh its value to the collection. The problem of securing an out-of-print book may often be solved by finding another title, perhaps one even more acceptable, to replace it. There are, however, some materials specifically needed by school libraries which are irreplaceable and should be ordered even at a higher price.

Remainders and Second-Hand Books

Remainders and second-hand books, as stated above, are often obtainable from the same dealers who carry out-of-print books. Remainders usually result either from overly optimistic publishing of a title or from overstocking the title by bookstores and other agencies which sell books. Except for occasional signs of having been handled, remainders are new books (in the sense that they have not been used) offered at reduced prices. Remainder lists frequently find their way to every school librarian's desk and prove a temptation. Local bookstores often have sales of remainders and book dealers occasionally issue remainder lists. Such lists should be checked promptly for desired titles and an order sent to the dealer as quickly as possible. The remainder trade may be helpful for the purchase of a title that is desirable but too expensive at the original price. Buying remainders is also an economical method of securing added copies of highly desirable titles. A word of warning, however, to school librarians: no book is a bargain unless it fills a real need in the collection, and remainders should be chosen with the same care as new books.

Second-hand books, of course, are those which have been used. They get into the trade when book dealers buy home libraries as estates are being settled, families move to smaller quarters, or the time for house cleaning arrives. Books no longer popular in rental libraries are often sold to second-hand book dealers. Once in a while one finds at second-hand bookstores discards from libraries or even books lifted from library shelves. Local dealers in used books are usually very cooperative about checking with libraries when a suspicious book turns up in a collection or is offered for sale.

One should buy a second-hand book only when it cannot be otherwise obtained. The book, having been used, is already in a weakened physical condition, and may soon need mending or rebinding. Second-hand books, especially if in demand, may also be offered at a price out of line with their value to a school library and the caution as to an understanding about the price before ordering out-of-print books applies as well to those bought second hand.

Names and addresses of dealers from whom out-of-print books, remainders and second-hand books are available may be obtained from advertisements in library periodicals. Advice as to which are considered good may be obtained from experienced librarians. The procedure for ordering such materials is the same as that outlined for ordering new books. On arrival in the library, such materials should be scrutinized carefully for satisfactory physical condition and to insure that the edition ordered is in hand. Books badly worn, in editions other than the one ordered, or otherwise unsatisfactory should be returned promptly.

Pamphlets

The *Vertical File Index*, available from the H. W. Wilson Company, may be used to advantage in ordering pamphlets. In the supplements to the *Children's Catalog* and *Standard Catalog for High School Libraries*, pamphlets are listed under the appropriate Dewey Decimal classification number following books listed for that number. Similar listing is not available in the main volumes because many pamphlets are kept in print only a short time. Pamphlets are included in other standard book selection aids and are often found in lists of free and inexpensive materials in both educational and library periodicals. The seventh edition of *Free and Inexpensive Learning Materials* prepared by the Division of Survey and Field Services of George Peabody College for Teachers (1956) is an example of mimeographed or printed lists appearing periodically. Another source for selection is *Pamphlets for Children's Library Collections*; "a selected list of free and inexpensive materials recommended for acquisition," compiled by Isabella Jinnette. Field Enterprises of Chicago also publishes a booklet, *Sources of Free and Inexpensive Educational Materials.* Full data on these sources will be found in the Appendix. The one drawback in using such sources is that the materials listed are often quickly exhausted so that the list is soon out of date.

Often pamphlets are obtainable free on request from publishers, industries, chambers of commerce and numerous other agencies. They should be requested immediately upon notice because the supply may be limited. Pamphlets which are of permanent value will probably be placed in pamphlet binders and treated as books while the more ephemeral pamphlets will find their way into the information file, as discussed in a later chapter.

Because most pamphlets must be obtained directly from the agencies responsible for issuing them, the simplest type of order is a printed or mimeographed card which may be mailed as a card or slipped into an envelope when stamps, taped-on coins, or a check must be enclosed. The same card may be used for both types of ordering, with the part which does not apply inked out. A form order card which might be used is illustrated by Figure 8.

```
Name of School
    Address                    '     Date_____

    Please send me a copy of _____

    _____

listed in _____

I enclose ___ cents to cover cost of same.
I assume this publication is free.  If not, please advise
    price before sending copy.

                            _____ Librarian
```

FIGURE 8
Card for ordering pamphlets

Government Publications

A few government publications, listed in standard book selection aids, are useful in any school library. Some of these are marked "gratis" and the price of others is usually reasonable. Other government documents are free upon request from state or national representatives, especially those newly elected with both time and a fresh quota of materials for distribution. School libraries interested in the purchase of Federal Government documents should write to the Superintendent of Documents, Washington 25, D.C., and ask to be put on the mailing list for *Selected United States Government Publications* and *Price List of Government Publications,* both available free. The procedure for ordering government documents would not be different from that already suggested for ordering books or pamphlets, since they appear in both forms. Like other specially printed materials, government documents have to be ordered direct, usually from the Superintendent of Documents, though in some instances from the issuing department. Money must accompany all orders for government documents except those that are gratis.

Magazines

Subscriptions to magazines may be ordered on a year-to-year basis, or on the "till forbidden" method which assures the continuance of the subscription until the library requests that it be stopped. For the school library, the magazine list should be reevaluated annually, with those titles dropped which have not proven their usefulness, or have outlived it, and new titles should be added. Before subscribing to a new magazine, it is wise to purchase several individual issues as "trial balloons" in order to gauge possible use of the title in the school library.

Selection should be made from lists of magazines included in book selection aids. The older editions of the *Standard Catalog for High School Libraries* carried a list of magazines prepared by the Magazine Evaluation Committee of the American Association of School Librarians, a list based on actual use. This service is no longer available, although there is a list of Catholic magazines in the Catholic supplement to the *Standard Catalog.* The *Basic Book Collection* series for elementary, junior high and senior high schools, referred to earlier in the chapter, all carry lists of magazines prepared by a special subcommittee of the Magazine Evaluation Committee mentioned above. *Magazines for School Libraries* by Laura K. Martin (H. W. Wilson, 1950), although now out of print and somewhat out of date, is still helpful for the evaluation of 100 older magazine titles.

Magazine subscriptions may run with the calendar year or begin with the school year in September, the latter probably being preferable for the school library. Though magazines are offered at reduced rates for the school year only, all issues should be subscribed for if the magazines are to be useful for reference purposes; otherwise, consideration might be given to a subscription for nine or ten months. Provisions should be made for the safe handling of magazines received during the summer months when the school library is usually closed.

Standards generally suggest an expenditure of 10 to 15 per cent of the school library appropriation for magazines and newspapers. However, no school librarian would consider this a hard and fast rule as so many factors enter into selection for school libraries. The number, as well as types, of magazines needed will vary from school to school according to the use made of magazines. Much less use of magazines, for instance, is made in elementary schools than in high schools, and there are fewer acceptable magazines available for the younger readers. On the high school level, many adult magazines are included for older readers. Each individual magazine title should be considered and selected on the basis of its contribution to the school library collection. In choosing magazines, as in book selection, the school librarian will consult with teachers as to the value of magazines in the school curriculum and will consider the reading interests of pupils in magazines intended for recreational purposes.

Generally speaking, the magazines to which a school library subscribes should be indexed in *Readers' Guide to Periodical Literature* or the *Abridged Readers' Guide*,[6] one of which every high school library should have if the magazines are to be used for reference. For the small library the *Abridged Readers' Guide* will suffice, but larger libraries will need the more extensive coverage of the *Readers' Guide to Periodical Literature*. While school libraries no longer bind many magazines, it is advised that all magazines subscribed for which are indexed in either index be kept for a period of three to five years for reference purposes.

The order form for magazines is not very different from that suggested for books. Any order for magazines constitutes a contract and should be paid for in full when the bill is presented, which is before the forthcoming issues are delivered. In case an issue fails to reach the school library, the agency handling the subscription should be notified to furnish a duplicate copy. Any copies missing after delivery to the school library must be replaced at the library's expense.

It is strongly urged that all magazines for the school library be ordered from a regular dealer. Reasons supporting such advice are almost parallel with those given for ordering books

[6] Subscriptions to the *Readers' Guide to Periodical Literature* (New York: H. W. Wilson Company) and the *Abridged Readers' Guide* (New York: H. W. Wilson Company) are sold on the service basis of charge.

from regular dealers. Saving in paper work and bookkeeping is effected; dealers are prepared to offer good discounts; and the library is assured of being supplied with duplicate copies of single issues which fail to arrive. Advice as to selection of a magazine dealer in the area may be obtained from other librarians. A librarian new on the job will do well, for the first year, to use the same dealer from which the school has been ordering magazines. F. W. Faxon of Boston and Mayfair of Englewood, New Jersey, are among the older reliable dealers in magazines.

Frequently there is a strong local appeal from someone who has a magazine subscription agency in the community. A local agent, however, cannot afford to give the best discounts and often the titles offered are in the form of magazine "clubs," which are never desirable for a school library. Another problem arises when a school group solicits subscriptions to magazines to raise money for a worth-while project and expects the school library to cooperate by ordering magazines for the library through the group. The fact that profits go to the project readily explains why little or no discount from the list price can be allowed. No school library should be pressured into submitting its subscription list of magazines to help finance a senior trip or purchase new uniforms for the band. The administrator can readily see that such practice is a case of "robbing Peter to pay Paul" and results either in fewer magazines for the school library or an extra appropriation to cover the loss of discount.

Audio-Visual Materials

Audio-visual materials for school use are handled in various ways. Some school libraries are set up as materials centers where are housed all types of teaching materials, including various forms of audio-visual materials. In other schools, the audio-visual materials are housed apart from the library, in the charge of a teacher. Many city and county systems have established centralized collections of audio-visual materials from which all schools in the system may borrow on demand or by a predetermined schedule, either through the school library or a teacher designated for such duties. Whatever the plan used, most school libraries cooperate in handling audio-visual materials, some of which, largely filmstrips and recordings, are part of the regular school library collection.

Though it now needs revision, the best guide to the treatment of audio-visual materials in the school library is *Audio-Visual School Library Service,* by Margaret Irene Rufsvold (American Library Association, 1949). Any school librarian who needs to work with audio-visual materials will certainly consult this book as well as other available materials on the subject. Attention is called also to the section in the sixth edition of *A Basic Book Collection for High Schools* entitled "Aids for Selection of Audio-Visual Materials and Equipment" [7] based on recommendations submitted by members of the audio-visual committee of the American Association of School Librarians.

The best aids for the selection of films and filmstrips are *Educational Film Guide* and *Filmstrip Guide.* Consult the Appendix for full references to audio-visual aids. Routines for ordering other types of materials can easily be applied to ordering audio-visual materials.

Pictures

Pictures for the picture collection lie somewhere between audio-visual materials and pamphlets and other materials for the information file. Usually pictures are obtained from sources at hand: magazines and books being discarded by the library, unsolicited advertising material reaching the librarian's desk, and contributions from teachers and pupils following a trip or resulting from a study project. Two commercial sources for pictures are Fideler Company, Grand Rapids, Michigan, and Keystone View Company, Meadville, Pennsylvania. Often there are notices or advertisements of pictures in educational and library periodicals. Where pictures are ordered from regular picture dealers or from an advertisement of special pictures available, order routines may be adapted from the suggestions made for ordering other types of materials.

[7] *A Basic Book Collection for High Schools* (Chicago: American Library Association, 1957) p. 135-6.

Gifts to the School Library

Gift materials bring problems which are probably more acute for school libraries than other types of libraries. The school library collection is relatively small, presumably chosen with great care, geared to the needs of a particular group, and usually displayed on open shelves in the reading room. Consequently, inclusion of a title in the collection implies approval, if not actual recommendation, to the readers. A general policy on gifts to the school library might well include the following points:

1. All materials should be accepted with the distinct understanding that the library may use it in accordance with the decision of the librarian in consultation with the faculty.

2. Material that obviously would not be acceptable in a school library should be refused outright. Examples are: old, out-dated books of non-fiction; good titles of fiction in poor editions that repel readers; unsuitable fiction such as series books, light love stories, sensational mysteries; and adult books with features questionable for use by adolescents.

3. School libraries should avoid "book showers" in which each pupil donates his favorite book, or members of the Parent-Teacher Association donate books from home collections. Some good material will undoubtedly be acquired by book showers but much poor material will also be donated.

4. It can be made clear that money is always more acceptable to school libraries than books chosen without relation to the school library collection. Where there is insistence on donating books, a list of desired titles, or at least of authors whose books would be acceptable, will direct choice in better channels.

5. Gift material should be acknowledged and credit given in library records. Publicity may be given to outstanding gifts that might encourage others to follow suit.

6. Special gift collections designed to be kept together should be discouraged, if not forbidden, in a school library. One high school library observed houses all books formerly in the personal library of one of its early graduates. Enclosed in cases with glass doors, the collection is neither ornamental nor useful, the bind-

ings being rather dull and the titles out-dated. Yet the collection occupies considerable space needed for shelving the present collection. Another school library possesses the complete works of a number of nineteenth-century poets and other similar material unsuitable for a school library—gifts from a prominent local family years ago—and seldom or never used.

7. Material received by gift which is standard yet not suitable for the school library should be offered elsewhere: to other school libraries of the area, to the local public library, or to a nearby college library.

8. Gift magazines often help to fill out missing numbers for magazine files or even to build a complete file of a title not subscribed to by the library, yet useful for reference. They also furnish material for the picture collection and/or information file. School librarians will be wise to accept as gifts to the magazine collection only titles recommended by standard aids and indexed in periodical indexes. A possible exception would be a local magazine with material not obtainable elsewhere. Magazines to be avoided even as gifts are: comics, magazines of the movie or true romance type, and those of a propagandistic nature.

Reinforced Bindings

Librarians find that books in regular trade bindings, as they come from the publishers, do not wear well under constant use. This is true especially with the present tendency to bind books in paper, or in paper with a cloth backstrip, imitation book cloth and other substitutes that last for only a few circulations. Because there is little time in a school library either for mending books, or supervising mending, and, because often only limited funds are available for rebinding books, school librarians look for other ways of assuring longer wear in books. One solution is to order prebound editions of those books which will receive hard wear, especially those for elementary readers. Some school libraries order prebound all books for use by grades one to three.

The summary of a statement (made in a letter to the author) from H. R. Huntting Company, booksellers and bookbinders, one of the oldest and largest dealers offering prebound books, will help explain the prebinding process. As far as possible, books from publishers are secured in sheets, folded and gathered, then sewed and cased in Class A heavy buckram bindings. Where it is the custom of publishers to bind the entire edition of any book printed, Huntting orders copies in bound stock, removes the covers and resews and recases the books in the type of binding mentioned above. The latter process is undoubtedly a waste of time and money, for which libraries eventually pay, and a solution to the problem is the concern of publishers, dealers, and librarians.

Huntting offers a service, available also from other dealers, whereby on request they will screen for libraries those books ordered which seem to need prebinding, supplying the others in trade bindings when these are substantial enough. This is a great service to school librarians who generally cannot examine books before purchase, as well as a saving to the library. Huntting will also accept standing orders for prebinding all books or those of a certain type. One elementary school librarian in the Bluegrass section of Kentucky, for instance, has a standing order that all books which mention horses must come prebound because of the popularity of "horse books" in the area. Other types of books to be prebound might be picture books, easy books and "teen-age" books.

Regular dealers also are handling more and more prebound books, in addition to those in trade bindings. For many years, A. C. McClurg and Company has offered books in prebindings as well as trade bindings. Baker and Taylor Company, mentioned earlier in this chapter with A. C. McClurg and Company as being the oldest and largest book dealers in the country, now supplies both trade bindings and prebound books. This service to the school library eliminates the necessity of submitting separate orders for books in the two types of bindings.

In addition to dealers who specialize in prebound books and regular dealers who also supply prebound books, attention is called to the fact that certain editions come direct from the publishers in stronger covers than the regular trade bindings. Any "school edition" of a book listed in book selection aids indicates that the binding has been reinforced. This is also true of "library binding," "library edition," "library bound covers," and other similar terms. Titles available in library bound editions are indicated in the publishers' catalogs. Care must be taken, when ordering, to specify that the stronger binding is desired. Many textbook publishers, however, provide firm bindings for books without indicating as much in their announcements. The main drawback is that the end product usually has the appearance of a textbook, and is not likely to be an attractive addition to the school library collection.

Harper and Brothers offers "reinforced library bindings." These cost less than prebound books because the binding used is book cloth rather than the Class A buckram which many librarians find often actually outwears the book which it binds. E. M. Hale and Company carries over three hundred titles, selected by an editorial board, in its Cadmus Books series which aims at providing "better binding at lower costs." One of their specialties is a reinforced edition of all the Landmark Books published by Random House. Don R. Phillips, Inc., has a variety of titles, including Landmark Books, in "Paragon Bindings"; the company, according to the catalog, strives to supply "the best prebound books on the market at the lowest prices." Follett Library Book Company announces in its catalog that with few exceptions all titles are "prebound in library bindings." There are undoubtedly many other examples of publishers' efforts to provide stronger bindings for books in school libraries.

When selecting a dealer, school librarians would do well to ascertain, among other facts, whether he can supply prebound books, what types of bindings are furnished, and at what price. In fact, a small trial order to several dealers simultaneously might serve as a means of comparing the kinds of prebound books supplied by each.

Time was when the cost of prebinding just about canceled any discount on a given book, so that the librarian usually figured the list price of the book as the actual cost of a prebound title. Now the cost of a prebound book is generally higher than the list price, though the longer wearing quality still justifies the expense.

Prebound books are in the long run still more economical than books which are purchased in trade bindings and rebound after library use. Furthermore, the school library does not have to do without those books which may be in heavy demand while they are out of circulation for rebinding. It might be added that binderies are equipped also to supply prebound books.

Junior Libraries has since November 1955 indicated by a letter code in its monthly book reviews the serviceability of the publisher's bindings—a helpful practice. In response to requests for more information as to how books are bound, prebound, or rebound, the issue of November 15, 1956, was largely devoted to a group of articles on bookbinding and the restoration and conservation of books,[8] containing much helpful and practical information.

A word of caution is necessary at this point. No book is worth the extra price of prebinding unless it is a valuable book in the first place. A prebound edition of a title should be ordered for its value to the collection, not merely because it is available. Selection of prebound titles should be made from standard book selection aids rather than from publishers' catalogs. Before going all out for books in reinforced bindings, school librarians should know what type of reinforcement has been used. This information may be obtained by correspondence, trial orders, visits to dealers wherever possible, and conferences with experienced librarians. Furthermore, books in reinforced bindings should be ordered as single titles rather than in groups as sometimes offered. The school library may otherwise receive much material not suitable for its own collection.

Conclusion

The acquisition of materials is a continuously interesting part of school library work. All materials should be selected from standard book selection aids, after consultation with teachers, in line with the reading abilities and interests of pupils in the

[8] *Library Journal.* 81:2701-12. November 15, 1956.

school, and with consideration of their value to the existing collection. Materials should be ordered from regular, authorized
dealers. Records, though simple, should at all times be kept in
such a way as to indicate the status of a book, or other item,
in process of acquisition, and should make clear the current expenditures in relation to the school library budget.

CHAPTER 2

PREPARATION OF MATERIALS FOR USE

Introduction

Success in the administration of a school library depends largely upon the careful preparation of materials for use. The processes should be simple, yet adequate, reduced to a routine easily followed by pupil assistants, and always performed in the same manner, regardless of who does what. The methods suggested in this chapter are based on procedures tried out in school libraries over the years and are today used in many school libraries.

Book Jackets

Most new books arrive in the library protected by book jackets or dust jackets, as they are sometimes called. These protective coverings are very colorful and many librarians like to retain them for use while the books are new. Books equipped with jackets are easily spotted on the shelves and lend a bit of color among older books that are drab and worn. Because the paper book jackets wear rather quickly, it is almost essential that they be covered with plastic material which, while offering protection, allows the book jackets to be seen. Plastic jackets to fit books of various sizes may be secured from library supply houses. The most recent offering is a plastic jacket which may be adjusted to fit books of several sizes. Plastic material obtainable in sheets may be cut to fit the book jacket and secured to the inside cover by a strip of mending tape.

If the book jacket is retained, the call number may be lettered directly on the spine of the jacket, as well as on the spine of the book itself, or a rectangular opening may be made in the book jacket to allow the call number on the spine of the book to be seen through the plastic cover. Both the book jacket and the protective plastic cover may be removed when the book is no longer

new, or when they themselves become worn. Then the cover of
the book itself is almost like new because it has been protected
through the first circulations.

Many school librarians find the above outlined process time-
consuming beyond its service to the library. Instead, they prefer
to remove the book jacket before starting a book on its journey
toward preparation for the shelves. A file of the most colorful
book jackets may be kept in the library for display purposes,
both to publicize newly acquired books and to use later with displays of books on certain subjects or by specific authors. Book
jackets may be kept filed by author, title, subject or call number.
Naturally, they can be filed by call number only after the corresponding books have been classified, so that the call numbers can
be put on the jackets. The system of filing used should be such
that the jackets may easily be located for maximum use in the
library or classrooms.

It is customary in many libraries to paste on the inside cover
of the book any picture of, and/or biographical material about,
the author which is found on the book jacket. In a school library,
however, this material would probably be more useful in the information file with other biographical material on authors, where
it will be available even when the book is in circulation.

School librarians are not unanimous about the advisability of
pasting in the book a clipping from the publisher's blurb found
inside the book jacket. Keeping such information with the book
helps the reader to know what the book is about, thus anticipating
the inevitable question the school librarian would otherwise have
to answer. Some teachers feel that there is enough information
in some excerpts from the book jackets to enable the pupil to
report on the book without having read it. A different type of
book report might here provide a solution. In any case, it is often
difficult to determine whether a book has actually been read because of the pupils' age-old custom of supplying information to
one another about the books they have been reading.

Book jackets from which material has been clipped, as suggested above, may still be used to cover new books or filed for

display purposes. If a clipped jacket is used to cover a new book, the plastic cover should extend well beyond the book jacket to hold it in place.

Opening New Books

Books newly arrived from the dealer should be opened properly before they are allowed to be handled. Otherwise, the book may be strained in the hinges by being forced open, thus resulting in the necessity for later mending or rebinding. The proper way to open a book is to hold the body of the book firmly in one hand while with the other each cover is laid flat on the table. Then the hinges which allow the covers to open and close should be pressed gently with the finger until the covers remain flat. Then, with each hand alternating, one continues to hold the body of the book upright while a group of pages, first on one side, then on the other, is pressed down at the hinges. When this process has been repeated until the center of the book has been reached, it should lie open flat on the table. If not, a repetition of the opening process with further pressing is indicated. This method should also be used with a book which is tight in its covers after rebinding.

Collating New Books

While the book is being opened in this manner, it should also be examined to see if any pages are missing, in the wrong order, or inverted, and if there are any other defects. This procedure is known in library work as collating the book. If examination shows any imperfection in the book, it should be laid aside to be returned to the dealer from whom it was purchased, so that a perfect copy may be supplied. A reliable dealer will replace an imperfect copy of a book even after it has been made a part of the library collection, but he will think better of the librarian if the book is returned beforehand. It is advised, therefore, that each book be collated as soon as possible after receipt in the school library.

Cutting Pages

The process of collating also includes watching out for uncut pages. These should be separated by a letter opener or other instrument with a dull edge. Otherwise, some future reader will perform this operation with his finger, a pencil, or a knife with sharp blade, any of which may damage the pages.

Entering the Trade Items

The trade items to be entered in a book consist of the source from which the book was ordered, date on which the entry is made, and price paid for the book. This entry is often referred to as the trade or business entry in the book and is entered from the order card as soon as possible after the book is collated. While the date of entry is usually included, it seems to serve no useful purpose and the busy school librarian would be justified in omitting it. In fact, many school librarians advocate omitting entirely the trade entry in the book itself. The source and price prove useful when the book is entered in the accession record. If the book happens to be a gift, the donor's name is given as the source and "G" or "gift" entered instead of the price.

There are variations, even among school libraries in the same system, as to where entries are placed in books, probably depending on where the librarians were trained. It is wise to use one page for all entries and the page following the title page seems a practical one for the purpose. Martha Wilson,[1] an early school librarian and writer about school libraries, suggested this among other simple methods of preparing books for use and many school librarians have since followed her example.

The trade items should be lettered in pencil about an inch from the bottom of the page parallel to the hinge of the book, far enough out to be easily read and so that the entry will not be destroyed if the book should later be rebound (Figure 9). The dollar mark is usually not placed beside the price. Since pupil assistants will probably enter the trade items, it will help in case of error to have each one sign his initials after the entry.

[1] Martha Wilson, *School Library Management*, 4th ed. (New York: H. W. Wilson Company, 1925)

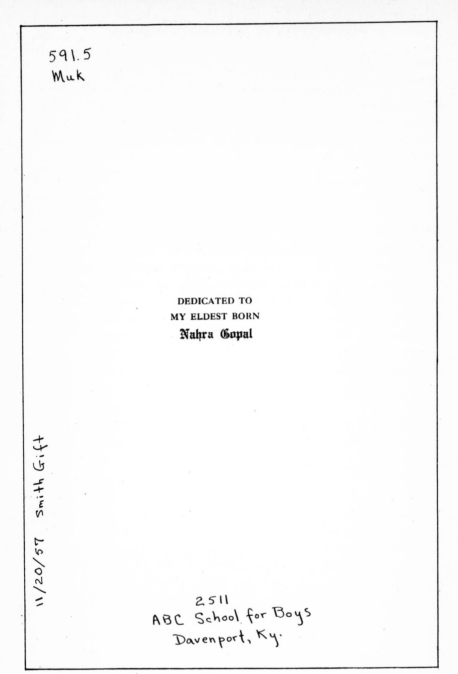

591.5
Muk

DEDICATED TO
MY ELDEST BORN
Nahra Gopal

11/20/57 Smith Gift

2511
ABC School for Boys
Davenport, Ky.

FIGURE 9
Page following title page on which are placed trade items etc.

The Accession Record

The accession record is made in a loose-leaf accession book purchased from any library supply house. The loose-leaf book should always be used because of convenience in typing and for ease in substitution should a page be spoiled and a new one need to be made.

Regardless of the number of accession sheets ordered, there are only two types available. One sheet is printed with numbers 01 to 50 and the other sheet with numbers 51 to 00. Books entered on the lines of the first two sheets take the numbers 1, 2, 3, etc., up to 100. Subsequent numbers are built up by placing the proper digit before the printed numbers, 101, 102, and so on. Care should be taken in building up numbers, as it is easy to skip an entire block of numbers, thus upsetting the correct count of books in the collection. It is sufficient to repeat the added digit only every five lines (Figure 10).

Accession Number

The accession number is very important in library work as it is the one mark which distinguishes each book from every other book in the collection. The accession number, as indicated above, is taken from the line on which the book is entered in the accession book, if one is used. Some school libraries note information usually obtained from the trade entry on the shelf-list card, as will be explained later, and thus do not use an accession book. In any event, the accession number indicates the order in which each book was added to the collection. This number is never used again, even after the book is finally discarded. Since the number is taken from the line on which the book is entered in the accession record, one entry must never run over to the line below because that carries a number which will belong to another book. Each item should be kept within the space provided for the purpose on its own line.

If an item is too long for the space, a decision should be made before the typing is begun as to whether the item is to be shortened or typed in two lines within the space. Initial articles in titles

Date   November 20, 1957

	Accession Number	AUTHOR TITLE
	2501	Adshead Inheritance of poetry
◯	02	A.C.E.I. Told under spacious skies
	03	Benna Europe since 1914
	04	Fenton Our changing weather
	05	" "
	2506	Harrer Seven years in Tibet
	07	Hatch General Ike
◯	08	Kantor Gettysburg
	09	" "
	10	Log-cabin lady
◯	2511	Mukerji Kari, the elephant
	12	Porter Scottish chiefs
	13	Previté-Orton Shorter Cambridge medieval
◯	14	" "
	15	Wilder By the shores of Silver Lake
	2516	Zim Trees
11/25/57	17	Collier's encyclopedia
	18	"
	19	"
	20	"
◯	2521	Collier's encyclopedia
	22	"
	23	"
	24	"
	25	"

FIGURE 10
Accession record

		PUBLISHER	YEAR	SOURCE	COST		REMARKS
		Houghton	1948	B & T	3	20	
		Macmillan	1952	"	2	40	
		Appleton	1954	"	4	40	
		Doubleday	1954	"	2	00	
		"	"	"		"	
		Dutton	1953	B & T	4	00	
		Holt	1952	"	2	40	
		Random	1952	"	1	20	
		"	"	"		"	
		Little	1922	"		"	
		Dutton	c1922	Smith	Gift		
		Scribner	1921	B & T	2	80	
history	v. 1	Cambridge	1952	"	10	00	2v.
	v. 2	"	"	"			
		Harper	1953	"	2	20	
		Simon & Schuster	1952	B & T	1	50	
	v. 1	Collier	1957	Direct	169	00	20v.
	v. 2	"	"	"			
	v. 3	"	"	"			
	v. 4	"	"	"			
	v. 5	Collier	1957	Direct			
	v. 6	"	"	"			
	v. 7	"	"	"			
	v. 8	"	"	"			
	v. 9	"	"	"			

may be omitted and accepted abbreviations used to conserve space. Dittos, one for each item, are permissible whenever the entry above is the same as the one being entered. In case of a set of books in many volumes, the appearance of the page is improved, however, by repeating the full entry every five lines (Figure 10).

Accession Entry

Each entry consists of the author's last name, brief title, publisher, date of book, source and price. If there is more than one author, only the last name of the author first mentioned on the title page of the book is entered in the accession entry. If no author is given on the title page, the entry is made alphabetically by the title which is entered in the space designated for the author and extends into the title space. The date, if given on the title page, is used in the accession entry; if not, the date is taken from the back or verso of the title page and a small "c" placed before the date to indicate that the copyright date is being used. The latest copyright date is used when there are more than one. If no date is given at either place, "n. d." is used to indicate that there is no date. The source and price are taken from the trade items in the book and pupil assistants should be instructed to enter in the accession book the source as it appears in the book. For instance, if the source given is C.B.E., that should be copied, even though the assistant knows that the initials stand for College Book Exchange. This is one of the reasons for having an accepted list of abbreviations available for the use of all those who work with school library records. In the case of a gift, as suggested earlier, the name of the donor appears as the source and either "G" or "gift" is entered instead of the price.

The date on which entries on each page are begun is placed in the space provided at the top. In case the page is not completed at one accessioning, the new date should be entered beside the first entry when the next accessioning is done. Each group of books to be accessioned at one time should be arranged in alphabetical order by author, or title where no author is given. This alphabetical arrangement assures that copies of the same book will be together for accessioning and that all volumes of a set are arranged in proper sequence. Some school librarians find that confusion results from having accession numbers of copies of the same book differ by only one digit. If this problem is felt to be acute, copies may be separated and accessioned at different times. This procedure should not be used in the case of sets of books, however. When a set of books is accessioned, the volume numbers should be entered in the space provided and the price of the entire set entered on the line for the first volume, with a notation of the total number of volumes beside the price to indicate that it is the cost of the entire set. The price is then not dittoed for each volume.

Periods, except to indicate abbreviations, are generally omitted from the accession record. When used, periods should be made lightly so as not to appear on the reverse of the sheet. In case a typewriter is not available, the accession record, being a permanent one, should be done neatly in ink, lettered if possible. Figure 10 shows the accession record made according to the above suggestions for the books received on the sample invoice in Figure 6.

As has already been suggested and will be discussed later, the accession record may be duplicated elsewhere in library records. For that reason, some libraries, especially those with large holdings, omit the accession record, keeping track otherwise of the accession numbers used. Since the accession number is necessary to distinguish any given book from all other books in the library collection, the accession number is used even when the accession record has been dispensed with. However, the accession book is recommended for the average school library. It is a fairly simple record which can be maintained even when the library must temporarily be in the hands of untrained personnel. One school librarian who had dispensed with the accession record to save time and duplication nevertheless arranged for the substitute during his year's leave of absence to keep an accession book and thus insure a correct record of books.

Use of Accession Number in Book

The accession number is lettered in ink, or stamped if the library owns a stamping machine, on the page following the title page where the trade entry was made. The accession number should be parallel to and about an inch from the bottom of the page, as nearly as possible in the center. Most libraries also enter the accession number on the secret page or key page, as it is sometimes called. The object of the secret page is to identify the book as belonging to a particular library when other marks of identification have been removed. However, since this record is less useful than others, the secret page might well be omitted in a school library. If used, a secret page fairly near the front should be selected since many books and pamphlets in a school library contain comparatively few pages. The accession number should be placed on the secret page, if one is used, in the same position as on the page following the title page. The accession number is used also on the book card and pocket, as will be explained later.

Classification

The books will need to be classified and call numbers assigned before they can be further prepared for the shelves. Classification is the librarian's responsibility because no one else can better judge where the book will be most useful to the collection. Teachers often request that certain materials on related topics be kept together because they are thus more easily located but this need can be met in other ways than by changes in classification. Subject headings in the card catalog will locate desired materials regardless of the classification number assigned but it is not wise to vary needlessly from the Dewey Decimal Classification.

School librarians are constantly urged not to attempt making the catalog cards until after a course in cataloging has been taken. However, classification numbers may be assigned before this course is taken if the person serving as librarian will consult the Dewey Decimal numbers suggested by the *Children's Catalog, Standard Catalog for High School Libraries* and other book selection aids which include classification numbers. The classification suggested by an outside source should not be accepted, however, until the librarian has checked his own catalog and shelf list to ascertain the previous practice of the library in cataloging books on the subject in question. If the title in hand is not included in any of the aids, as often happens in the case of an old book or a less well-known title, at least a tentative classification number may be obtained from the section in the *Children's Catalog* or *Standard Catalog for High School Libraries* devoted to other books on the same subject. For example, a book about stars will be classified in 523.8 regardless of the author, publisher, or copyright date. A copy of the abridged edition of *Dewey Decimal Classification & Relative Index* [2] will also be essential when the school librarian undertakes to assign classification numbers. Another useful tool in classification is the latest edition of *Sears List of Subject Headings* published by the H. W. Wilson Company. This list is essential in selecting subject headings when books are cataloged but it also suggests classification numbers.

It is not recommended that pupils, parents, or other untrained assistants attempt to classify books, even though such procedure is suggested by some books on school library work. Classification is difficult even for the experienced librarian, when the process is considered, as it should be, as being more than just selecting a number from a list and assigning it to a book.

The Call Number

The call number of a book is composed of the classification number and the author or book number. Larger libraries, where it is more necessary to distinguish between call numbers, use the author's initial, a number from the Cutter table (named for the man who worked out the system of numbers in place of names) and the first letter of the title to complete call numbers. Thus, the full call number for *A Basic History of the United States* by Charles Austin Beard and Mary Ritter Beard would be $\frac{973}{B38b}$. The 973 is, of course, the Dewey number for United States history.

[2] Melvil Dewey, *Decimal Classification & Relative Index*, abridged (7th) ed. (Lake Placid Club, New York: Forest Press, 1953)

The first "B" is for Beard, 38 is the Cutter number for the authors' name, and "b" is from the first word, not an article, of the
title, *Basic*. The use of Cutter numbers is not recommended for
school libraries except possibly the very large ones used by senior
high school students, and school librarians in the average library
are warned against starting their use.

Most school libraries, especially the smaller ones, use only
the initial of the name of the author first mentioned on the title
page to complete the call number. Thus, using this simple form,
the call number for the above book would be $\frac{973}{B}$ and a book about
birds by Matthews would be $\frac{582}{M}$. This practice suffices as long as
the collection remains small and there is not much chance that
there will be many books with identical call numbers. However,
with this system being used in larger school library collections, it
is difficult to keep books in alphabetical order on the shelves because the call number of a book of United States history by Bates,
Beard, Billings, or Burke would each be $\frac{973}{B}$.

A simple solution is to use the first three or four letters of the
author's name. In fact, some school librarians use up to five letters because many names are completed within that number.
Still others advocate the use of the author's entire name where
width of the book's spine permits. Thus if the library were using
four letters, the Beard book would have for a call number $\frac{973}{Bear}$
and the book by Matthews $\frac{582}{Matt}$, a practice which would allow
books to stand on the shelves in more nearly correct alphabetical
order within each classification.

Attention of the uninitiated in classification is called to the
fact that in individual biography the initial of the name of the
person about whom the book is written is used instead of the author. The reason for this is to insure that all biographies of the
same person will stand together on the shelves. Thus any biography of Washington would have for a call number $\frac{B}{Wash}$ regardless
of who wrote the book. This scheme, it is true, makes no distinc-
tion in the call number between a book about Booker T. Washington, for instance, and a biography of George Washington, nor
between a biography of George Washington written by Foster or
one by Hill. For this reason, some school librarians use Cutter

numbers for individual biography even when they are not used for any other books in the collection. However, this is not advised for the average school library where duplications in call numbers of individual biographies will not be excessive. Besides, one easily distinguishes books by title when finding them on the shelves; in fact, young readers seek titles almost exclusively in using the library.

The classification number used for individual biography is a source of concern to many school librarians. Most libraries designate individual biography with B as indicated above, and shelve the books following the 900 classification. In the early editions, 921 was used by the *Children's Catalog* and the *Standard Catalog for High School Libraries* to designate individual biography. As a result, individual biography in shelving followed 920, collective biography, in natural sequence. Pupils, having learned that zero in the Dewey Decimal System stands for general works, easily distinguish between 920, lives of many persons, and 921, which designates the biography of only one person.

The number 92 now used by the above-mentioned book selection aids is less satisfactory because it is different in number of digits from other numbers and is somwhat awkward to handle in lettering. There is also a problem of whether to shelve 92 before or after 920. As a solution, it is advised that school libraries use 921 for individual biography even though the number is not now in use in standard aids.

The practice of using F for fiction is fairly general in school libraries. The call number for one of Alcott's novels would be $\frac{F}{Alco}$ and for a novel by Elizabeth Janet Gray, $\frac{F}{Gray}$. One school librarian dispenses with the F and letters the full name of the author on the spine of each book of fiction at the place where the call number usually appears. This may consume some more time in lettering but pays off in shelving or locating books on the shelves and makes pupils more conscious of authors. The corresponding catalog and book cards then have no call numbers, indicating that the book is fiction and should be located under the author's name. Neither scheme, of course, distinguishes among titles of fiction books by the same author. A white line drawn under the title on the spine of each book will help to call attention to the title, after the reader has located the desired author.

Call Number in the Book

After the call number has been assigned to a book, it is lettered in pencil in the upper left hand corner of the page following the title page where the trade items and accession number have already been placed (Figure 9). It should be about an inch from the top of the page and far enough from the inner margin so that it will not be cut off when the book is later rebound. This becomes the official call number to be entered on the book card and book pocket, as well as on the spine, and on catalog cards for the book.

Book Cards and Pockets

When book cards are ordered for use in school library work, the type that includes space for the pupil's home room number, as well as his name, is recommended. This record, made at the time the pupil takes the book out, saves valuable time when notices for overdue books or fines must be sent.

On the first line of the card, the call number of the book is placed at the left and the accession number on the right. If the book is one of a set, the volume number should be used as part of the call number. It is not recommended that copy numbers be used when there are several copies of the book, since the accession number distinguishes each individual volume from all others. Above the accession number should be noted the cost of the book, copied from the trade entry. It is a great convenience to have this information on the card when the book is missing. Often the reader is prepared to pay for a lost book but the assistant cannot leave the desk to consult the accession record for the price. This practice is strongly recommended for all school libraries. On the second line is typed the author's last name, preferably in capital letters, and on the line below the brief title of the book (Figure 11).

```
551.59
Fent                                    2504
AUTHOR

FENTON
TITLE
Our changing weather
```

DATE DUE	BORROWER'S NAME	ROOM NUMBER
	GAYLORD 65	

Book card
FIGURE 11

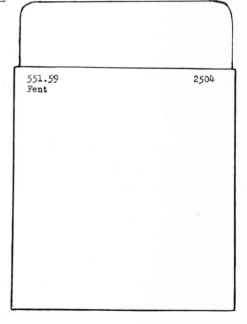

FIGURE 12
Book pocket

```
551.59                                  2504
Fent
```

Book pockets for school libraries should be the kind that is reinforced across the top. These may be ordered from any library supply house. Small readers insist on depositing pennies for fines in the book pocket, then insert their hands to retrieve the pennies, a procedure which soon tears the pocket that is not reinforced across the top. The book pocket carries the call number on the left and the accession number on the right in the same position as on the book card so that checking while replacing the card in the pocket will be simple (Figure 12). It is not actually necessary to repeat the author's name and the title of the book on the book pocket and school librarians are not advised to spend time doing so. As a time-saving device, the book card may be inserted in the pocket before it is rolled into the typewriter and the information typed first on the card, then on the book pocket. This arrangement also insures more accuracy in getting correct information on the card and pocket.

If a typewriter is not available, information should be lettered or written neatly with waterproof ink on the book card and pocket. If the information is typed, the book card and pocket should be prepared when the book is cataloged.

Pasting in Pockets and Date-Due Slips

The pocket is pasted on the inside back cover of the book, as nearly in the center as possible. While the four fingers of the left hand are held inserted in the pocket, paste is applied around the edges of the back side of the pocket. With the fingers still inside, the pocket is applied to the inside cover of the book and held in place with the right hand until the left can be removed. This prevents getting paste on the hands. Then, with a paste cloth, excessive paste is removed and the pocket pressed firmly into place. After the pocket has been allowed to dry, the book card may be safely inserted.

The date-due slip is pasted on the last page in the book, usually the fly leaf, opposite the book pocket, placed as nearly in the center as possible (Figure 13). Date-due slips arrive from any library supply house with a narrow band of gummed surface

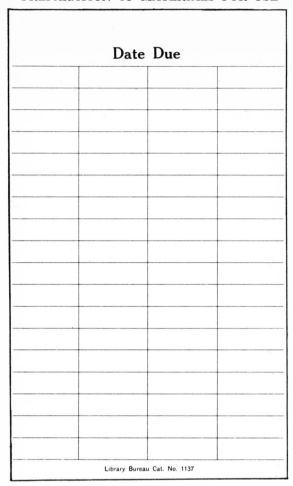

FIGURE 13
Date-due slip

across the top on the back. It is advised that this be moistened with paste, rather than water, because the gum alone is not sufficient for holding. For ease in removing when the date-due slip is filled up and must be replaced, paste should not be applied lower than the gummed strip. In case there is reading material on the last page of the book, the date-due slip should be pasted across the top margin of the page so that the reader can still read the printed lines beneath the date-due slip.

Some librarians advocate pasting the book pocket and date-due slip in the front of the book but no particular advantage seems to result from this practice. Since the charging equipment adds nothing to the attractiveness of the book, the back of the book is recommended as the place to insert it.

Lettering the Books

Before books are finally ready for the shelves, it is necessary to letter the call number on the spine of each book. The number should be lettered far enough up on the spine to be above the publisher's name, which is usually printed near the bottom of the spine, yet not so high as to obscure the title or the author's name. Two inches from the bottom is a very good distance; whatever is chosen should be the same on all books. Such a practice makes books easier to shelve and look better once they have been placed on the shelves. The simplest way to determine distance is to fold a 3″ by 5″ card the desired distance from one end of the card making an L-shaped angle. When the long arm of the angle is held flat against the bottom of the book, the top of the other arm on the spine will indicate where the classification number is to be placed. The second line of the call number is placed below the classification number after the measuring card has been removed. The size of letters and figures making up the call number should be gauged according to the size of the book.

Library pens and lettering ink are available from any library supply house. The type of pen will depend largely on the preference of the person doing the marking. White ink should always be secured from a library supply house and must be replaced often because it thickens and cannot be successfully thinned. For that reason only one bottle should be purchased at a time. Call numbers should be lettered in white ink on dark books and in black waterproof ink on light colored books. When the book cloth is rough, or otherwise of such a nature that ink will run, the space on the spine where lettering must go should have a coat of shellac applied to it. After the shellac has dried, ink may be used without danger of running.

Gadgets are sold for holding the book in place during the process of lettering. A simple but effective method, however, is to sit at a desk which has a drawer on the left side. The book is placed in the drawer with spine up and the drawer closed against the book. The drawer holds the book in place, thus releasing both hands for the lettering process.

A card demonstrating types of lettering for books is available from library supply houses. Whoever letters books for the school library should practice until a smooth, readable type of lettering has been achieved. Nothing mars the appearance of books on the shelf more than poor lettering placed at all angles on the spine.

When printing on the spine does interfere with the space chosen for the call number, one of two methods may be used. The call number may be placed either above or below the printed material on the spine. Or a band of black may be applied where the call number belongs and allowed to dry before lettering is done. Some libraries use india ink for this purpose. A better solution to this problem is a mixture of shellac and powdered lamp black, a full teaspoonful of the latter to a cup of shellac kept in a container with a tight-fitting top. Lamp black may be obtained very cheaply from any hardware store and shellac is standard equipment in all libraries. This mixture furnishes a smoother surface than india ink and is more easily applied since a brush is used. A black band can also be used to cover a call number which has been spoiled in lettering or needs to be changed for any reason. Some libraries advocate using the black band for all books, though it is not recommended for school libraries. While the white lettering stands out well on the smooth black surface, the process consumes more time than it is worth.

Some librarians prefer lettering done with one of the types of electric stylus offered by library supply houses. By means of heat applied to a special colored transfer paper or gold transfer foil, the call number is lettered on the spine of the book. The stylus is plugged into any electric outlet of the standard 110-volt type, alternating or direct current. The hot point of the stylus will also remove the lettering in case an error is made.

Also available commercially is a device for lettering by following a model of perfect letters and figures. The device reproduces whatever is traced by means of an extended arm to which a pen is attached. However, the lettering can be done only on labels, which are not recommended for use in school libraries. Children will pick at anything which can be detached and the librarian would have to be constantly replacing labels.

Many books and practically all pamphlets are too thin to allow lettering of the call number across the spine. There are two ways of lettering these materials. Where the spine will allow, the call number may be lettered along it instead of across it. One should begin the lettering at a distance of more than two inches from the bottom of the spine and work down. This distance should be the same for all books so lettered and it is suggested that the longer side of the 3″ by 5″ card, folded to measure two inches on other books, is a good distance for lettering thin books. Or the call number may be lettered on the front cover of the book, either two inches from the bottom or near the top of the book, in either case close to the hinge. Lettering at the top will enable the call number to be seen without removing the book entirely from the shelf.

Applying Shellac

After the book is lettered, it is necessary to protect lettering with shellac. It is especially important that lettering done in white ink never be handled until the shellac has been applied, as the white ink will smear or rub off altogether. Tests show that it takes no more time and probably very little more shellac to cover the entire spine than to make a successful job of covering just the space where lettering has been done. Consequently, shellacking the entire spine is recommended both for new books and for old books which need to be freshened in appearance. When lettering is done on the front cover, shellac should be applied only over the lettered surface, in a rectangular shape. Many school librarians find it advisable to shellac the entire cover of books that are very light in color or otherwise vulnerable to soiled hands. After shellacking, the cover may be wiped off with a slightly damp cloth when the book has become soiled.

Clear or white shellac may be obtained from any library supply house and mixed in equal proportions with shellac thinner for ease in applying. This mixture should be applied with a brush. A container for shellac with a device to hold the brush when not in use is convenient. Shellac thickens quickly but may be thinned with shellac thinner, which may also be used to keep at the right consistency the mixture of lamp black and shellac mentioned earlier. There is available a clear plastic spray for shellacking books, but librarians who have used it find this method expensive, both because of the initial price and the unavoidable waste of sprayed material.

Shellacking of books is probably best done just before the library closes, to prevent danger of handling books before they have had a chance to dry overnight. Books freshly shellacked should be placed so as not to touch each other and with the spine extending over the edge of shelf or table in the work room. Another convenient method is to suspend the books, spine up, over a stout cord stretched between two chairs. It injures books to place them half opened and face down. A further caution is added against handling books before the sticky shellac has dried.

Marks of Ownership

Each school library should have a rubber stamp with its name to be stamped on the books for identification. The stamp should be placed on the page following the title page under the accession number and in the same place on the secret page, if one is used. It also should be placed across the bottom of the book pocket. Since there should be some sign that the book is ready to be shelved, it is suggested that the stamp across the bottom of the pocket designate this. Some libraries like to use the stamp also on the edges of the body of the book, as a further means of identification and as an added measure to discourage the disappearance of books from the school library shelves.

Shelving Books

Properly shelved, books should occupy only two thirds of each shelf to give room for expansion. One can shelve about eight ordinary-sized books to a running foot, and from ten to twelve thinner books such as are found in elementary school libraries. To house picture books, which are likely to be tall and thin, in orderly fashion, the height between shelves should be twelve inches with a thin partition about every six to nine inches on the shelves. Library shelves except those for picture books should always be adjustable so that they may be moved to accommodate oversize books.

Books should be arranged on the shelves from left to right by the call number. The spines of the books should be flush with the edge of each shelf. A metal book support will be necessary for each shelf to assure that the books will stand upright. If the shelf becomes full, the book support may be placed behind the row of books so as to be readily available when books go out and the support is again needed. Shelf labels with classification number and subject headings will assist in locating books more quickly. Metal holders for labels may be ordered from a library supply house. The type of holder which slips over the shelves is advised. Fixed shelf labels should be avoided, because of the necessity for frequent shifting of books from one shelf to the other.

Because the sections which house books of fiction are used more often than non-fiction, thus causing crowding about the shelves, some school librarians have found it helpful to employ the "ribbon arrangement" for fiction. This scheme places fiction on the top shelf, for instance, of all sections of shelves, with books of non-fiction arranged in regular order below the fiction. Often this increases reading of non-fiction, as readers find books of interest while looking for fiction.

Open shelves are recommended whenever possible for use in school libraries. Stacks discourage the use of books and increase discipline problems and the need for supervision. If shelves other than those flat against the wall must be used in the reading room, they should be placed so that the spaces between sections of shelving can be supervised easily.

Making Catalog Cards

Somewhere in the process of preparing books for the shelves, cards must be made for and filed in both the card catalog and the shelf list. The process of learning to prepare catalog cards, whether there are printed cards available for the book or the cards must be typed, constitutes a separate course in the library science curriculum. Consequently, no attempt is made here to teach cataloging or to offer short-cuts to simplify the cataloging process. If a school library is to provide maximum service to pupils and teachers, a good card catalog is of prime importance. It has already been advised and is again emphasized that school librarians purchase printed cards whenever available and type cards only for those books for which printed cards cannot be obtained. School librarians are also advised not to attempt to catalog materials until after a course in cataloging has been taken. A school library can function for a time without a card catalog if the books are classified and equipped for circulation. Making catalog cards is a technical process and when attempted by an amateur the task usually has to be done again. That is the reason for suggesting that the order cards may serve as a temporary shelf list until cataloging has been done, since the shelf list is indispensable.

Shelf List

It is necessary here, however, to give some consideration to the shelf list. This record consists of one card for each title in the library. The cards are filed by call number so that they stand in the drawer in the same order in which the books stand on the shelves. The shelf list is kept convenient to the desk where cataloging is done, usually in the work room or librarian's office, and is not for use by the readers.

The shelf list is valuable for indicating quickly the number and types of books in the library's holdings in each division of the Dewey Decimal Classification. It is helpful in acquainting a new school librarian with the library collection. The shelf list is consulted during the process of classification and cataloging to insure that the cataloger is consistent in the use of classification numbers. It also serves as a record of the final disposition of each book and is an indispensable tool in taking inventory.

Each shelf-list card is a duplicate of the main or author card catalog except that notes and/or contents are omitted from Wilson catalog cards intended for the shelf list and from those that are typed in the library. This is necessary in order to leave space beside the accession number to enter record of the final disposition of each book (Figure 14a). When an added copy of a book already in the library is being prepared for the shelves, the accession number of the new copy is added to the shelf-list card.

```
551.59
Fen    Fenton, Carroll Lane
              Our changing weather, by Carroll Lane Fenton
        and Mildred Adams Fenton.    Doubleday ₁1954₁
              110 p. illus.


2504
2505
```

FIGURE 14a

Shelf-list card when accession record is used

However, a new edition of any title, especially of non-fiction, is considered another book and a new set of cards, including the shelf-list card, should be made.

By comparing the two records, it can plainly be seen that the shelf-list card contains all the information about a book which is in the accession record except the source and date of acquisition. Consequently, some libraries which no longer keep the accession

```
551.59
Fen    Fenton, Carroll Lane
            Our changing weather, by Carroll Lane Fenton
       and Mildred Adams Fenton.    Doubleday [1954]
            110 p. illus.

2504   B & T   11/25/57   2.00
2505     "        "         "
```

FIGURE 14b

Shelf-list card when accession record is not used

book, as mentioned earlier, enter the trade items beside the accession number for each book on the shelf-list card (Figure 14b). Since the record of what happens to each book must be kept on the shelf-list card, even when an accession book is used, it is not advised that the busy school librarian duplicate this by entering it also in the "remarks" column of the accession book.

Such notations as "Lost and paid 1958" or just "Lost 1958" or "Missing in inventory 1958" or "Discarded 1958" should be entered lightly in pencil beside the accession number of each book on the shelf-list card, as occasion demands. To save time, school librarians should work out a reasonable code of abbreviations for such entries. When a book cannot be located on the shelf and is apparently not in circulation, the shelf list should indicate any known reason why the book is not available. After the book is missing for a reasonable time, notation should be entered on the shelf-list card. The problem of withdrawing books from the collection is discussed in Chapter 6. It should be noted here, however, that the shelf list is a fairly permanent record and that each card should be retained even after the title it represents is no longer in the school library collection. Where there are a number of cards for withdrawn books, they may be removed from the shelf list for books in use and put in another place. If the school librarian finds no use for "withdrawn" shelf-list cards, they may be discarded after a reasonable time.

Newspapers

The average school library subscribes to so few newspapers that a checking record is hardly necessary, though cards for the purpose are available from library supply houses. Each day, as the newspapers arrive, the previous issue should be removed from, and the new one put on, the newspaper holder. Before any newspapers are put out, single pages should be attached in place either by paste along the inner edge or by a hinge of mending tape. The type of newspaper holder which is split into sections and secured at the end by a rubber ring is suggested for school library use. More than one issue of a newspaper may be accommodated on this type of file when there is need for back issues. Any holder with a nail or other sharp instrument to hold the newspaper tends to tear the paper and is not recommended for school use. Used newspapers should be clipped for the information file before being discarded.

Magazines

When a new issue of a magazine arrives in the library, it should be checked as soon as possible in the Kardex file for magazines, obtainable from any library supply house. Each title is represented, in alphabetical order, by two cards, one bearing the permanent record of source, price, binding, etc., and the other serving as the checking record (Figures 15 and 16). Monthly magazines may be checked in the correct space to indicate arrival. However, if it seems helpful to readers to know when the new issue will arrive, the date received may be used in the checking record. In the case of weekly magazines, it is well to enter on the checking record the date of each issue received. A small school library which subscribes to only a few magazines may prefer to keep a simpler file of magazine cards for checking issues as they

YR VOL.	1	2	3	4	5	6	7	8	9	10	11	12	13	14	15	16	17	18	19	20	21	22	23	24	25	26	27	28	29	30	31	T.P.	I.
JANUARY																																	
FEBRUARY																																	
MARCH																																	
APRIL																																	
MAY																																	
JUNE																																	
JULY																																	
AUGUST																																	
SEPTEMBER																																	
OCTOBER																																	
NOVEMBER																																	
DECEMBER																																	

BOUND   AT BINDERY

INCOMPLETE   BIND

VOLS. PER YEAR   NOS. PER VOL.

TITLE PAGE & INDEX
NONE
SEND FOR
LOOSE
LAST NO.
NEXT VOL.

INC.

DESTINATION

TYPIST PLEASE NOTE — THIS SCALE CORRESPONDS TO (PICA) SCALE — SET PAPER GUIDES SO THAT CARD SCALE WILL REGISTER WITH MACHINE SCALE WHEN CARD IS TURNED INTO WRITING POSITION   START INDEX (3) POINTS FROM LEFT EDGE OF CARD, USE OTHER POINTS OF SCALE FOR OTHER DIVISIONS OF VISIBLE TITLE, SET TABULATORS TO INSURE PERFECT ALIGNMENT OF EACH DIVISION OF INFORMATION.   FOLD BACK OR REMOVE STUB AFTER TYPING.   USE NEW TYPEWRITER RIBBON.

KARDEX
VISIBLE   347-876 C   REMINGTON RAND BUSINESS SERVICE INC.
DIVISION   PRINTED AT   TONAWANDA, N. Y.   U. S. A.

FIGURE 15
Checking card from Kardex file

arrive (Figures 17a & b). If there is time to prepare it, a checking chart hung conspicuously near where magazines are housed will let readers know at a glance whether a new issue has arrived. (See Figure 18 for suggested form.) The checking record in the Kardex file should be gone over frequently for issues of magazines that have failed to arrive so that the agent may be notified promptly to supply duplicate copies. In a school library, readers will keep the librarian aware that certain magazines are missing, but one cannot depend on this for those not used a great deal.

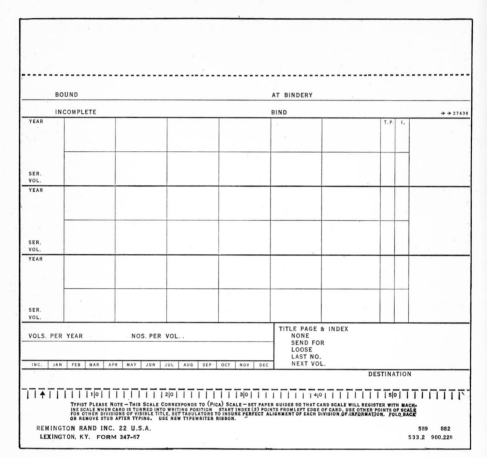

FIGURE 16

Card for binding record in Kardex file

The name of the library should be stamped on the magazine on both the front and back covers, always in the same place, and on the same secret page, if one is used, as for books. The date on which the magazine is received in the library should also be stamped on the front cover, probably near the upper right-hand corner. If the library circulates non-current issues of magazines, "Do Not Circulate" should be stamped in the upper left-hand corner of the back cover of each magazine being prepared for use. Further discussion of this routine will be found in Chapter 3 on circulation. This is important because the latest issue of any magazine should be used only in the library where all readers will have a chance to read it.

Name										Due			
Year	Vol.	Jan.	Feb.	Mar.	Apr.	May	June	July	Aug.	Sept.	Oct.	Nov.	Dec.	T.P.&I.

No. Copies   Depts.   Indexed in

(OVER)

FIGURE 17a
Checking card for magazine

(Publisher's name)   (Publisher's address)
List price   Vols. begin   Bind

Ordered of..Date................Expires................Cost...................
Ordered of..Date................Expires................Cost...................
Ordered of..Date................Expires................Cost...................
Ordered of..Date................Expires................Cost...................
Ordered of..Date................Expires................Cost...................
Ordered of..Date................Expires................Cost...................
Ordered of..Date................Expires................Cost...................
Ordered of..Date................Expires................Cost...................
Ordered of..Date................Expires................Cost...................
Ordered of..Date................Expires................Cost...................

Short   1st Notice sent   2nd Notice sent   3rd Notice sent

GAYLORD 35Y   PRINTED IN U.S.A.

FIGURE 17b
Checking card for magazine (reverse)

Checking Record for Magazines (to be displayed near magazine rack)

Title of magazine	Comes	Sept.	Oct.	Nov.	Dec.	Jan.	Feb.	Mar.	Apr.	May	June	July	Aug.
American Girl	M	✓											
Boys' Life	M	✓											
Business Week	W	✓											
Current History	M	✓											
Good Housekeeping	M	✓											
Harper's Magazine	M	✓											
National Geographic	M	✓											
Nature Magazine	M	✓											
Sat. Evening Post	W	✓											
Scientific American	M	✓											
Senior Scholastic	W	✓											
U.S. News and World Report	W	✓											

FIGURE 18

Checking record for magazines

Reinforcement of Magazines

Before magazines are put out for use in school libraries, they should either be reinforced or placed in protective covers. The older types of solid binders for magazines are not recommended for use in school libraries. These binders are expensive, hide the attractive magazine covers and also disguise the fact that the magazine itself may be missing. Strong plastic covers are available from library supply houses or advertised in library periodicals by such companies as Marador and Bro-Dart Industries. The librarian should try several types before ordering in quantity.

Some librarians report that reinforcement by sewing, where magazines are held together by saddle sewing or stapling, helps to preserve magazines even when kept in binders, or covers. Later, if and when magazines are circulated from the library, this reinforcement helps to prolong their period of use.

If binders or covers are not used, then it is absolutely necessary to reinforce magazines. The simplest method is to resew the thin magazines through the center of the spine. Some librarians remove the magazine cover, line it with tough paper, then replace the contents in the cover by sewing. A strip of Mystik tape, available from library supply houses, will cover sewing on the outside and make a neat finish. Or a strip of hinge tape used inside each of the hinges will help to reinforce the magazine. For magazines like the *National Geographic* which have firm side sewing or stapling and a flat rather than a rounded spine, the cover may be carefully removed, then put back with a strip of double-stitched binding of correct width. The method of using double-stitched binding in repairing is discussed in Chapter 5.

Magazines are best displayed on sloping shelves designed for the purpose. Underneath each sloping shelf, a flat shelf will hold several back issues of the same magazine. For ease in locating and replacing magazines, they should be arranged alphabetically by title with appropriate labels. If magazines are housed in a magazine rack where they must stand in an upright position, wire holders obtainable from library supply houses will be necessary to prevent the smaller magazines from dropping out of sight in space provided for taller ones. The housing of back issues for reference purposes will be discussed in Chapter 5.

Information File Material

The file of material designed to supplement the book collection is called the "Information File" because of its purpose and "Vertical File" because it is housed in upright cabinets. It should be housed in files of legal size, preferably with four drawers. These files should be equipped with ball bearings for ease in operation of drawers when heavy with materials. In the file are placed pamphlets that are not to be cataloged, leaflets, clippings and other materials which may serve to supplement the book collection. As stated earlier, those pamphlets which are considered of sufficient value to be made part of the book collection are put into pamphlet binders, classified and cataloged, and otherwise treated in preparation like books. Although material placed in the information file will not be as permanent as that cataloged, care in selection must still be used.

For pamphlets and other materials that are separates, the process of preparation is fairly simple. Each is stamped with the name of the library, following the routine suggested for magazines. If there is a date on the pamphlet or clipping, this should be circled with a colored pencil to call attention to date. Otherwise, the date on which the material is placed in the file should be stamped on the material. This date helps a great deal in determining the continuing value of each piece when the vertical file is "weeded."

A subject heading is lettered in pencil in the upper right-hand corner of the pamphlet or other material as it will stand in the file. For conformity of subject headings, it is wise to follow a standard list, checking those subject headings used in the file and inserting others which are used but are not in the printed list. The *Pamphlet File in School, College and Public Libraries* [2] is suggested as a useful subject headings list for school libraries, though larger high school libraries may wish to use *Subject Headings for the Information File*, [3] which is based on subject headings used in the Newark, New Jersey, Public Library.

[2] Norma Olin Ireland, *Pamphlet File in School, College and Public Libraries*, rev. and enl. ed. (Boston: F. W. Faxon Company, 1954)

[3] *Subject Headings for the Information File*, ed. by Miriam Ogden Ball, 8th ed. (New York: H. W. Wilson Company, 1956)

Pamphlets and other materials on the same subject should be kept together in a manila folder on which the subject has also been typed or lettered. In cases where there are multiple copies of a pamphlet for classroom use, one copy only should be kept in the vertical file with space allotted elsewhere, probably in the storage or work room, for other copies. A notation on the front cover of the copy in the file can be used to indicate how many copies are available elsewhere.

Clippings

The school librarian will check with colored pencil in newspapers, magazines, and books which are being discarded any articles to be clipped by pupil assistants. Persons clipping material should be instructed always to clip the entire article and fasten parts together with a paper clip. At once the source and date of the material should be entered at the top of the clipping. If there is no space in which to pencil this information, it should be written on a small slip of paper and pasted to the clipping. Nothing is more annoying than to find missing a part of a useful clipping or to read an article on atomic energy with no indication as to whether it was written in the current year or ten years earlier.

For use in school libraries, it is advised that clippings be pasted down wherever possible as they are easily misplaced when loose and often cannot be replaced. Odds and ends of heavy paper and lightweight cardboard of varying sizes should be saved for this purpose. If the clipping is too long for one side of the mount, the pasting down process may be continued on the back. The subject heading is then lettered on the mount in the upper right hand corner as each will stand in the file. After the clipping has dried under weight, it is placed in a manila folder as suggested for pamphlets.

In the case of clippings of several pages, especially if needed material is on both sides of each page, pasting down is obviously not the solution. It is advised instead that each clipping be stapled or pasted across the top in a manila folder and that the subject heading be lettered on the guide tab of the folder. Thus there will be uniformity in the file, regardless of size or type of material included.

As was suggested for pamphlets, only those clippings should be kept that give promise of usefulness. The vertical file is not intended to be a "catch-all" and time should not be spent in preparing worthless material. The file should supplement, rather than duplicate, the book collection. Any school librarian will soon learn what subjects are called for often—local history, authors, especially recent ones, careers—and can better be supplied from the information file. Each mount should have the library stamp and the date added to the file, as suggested for pamphlets. It is not advised that vertical file material be accessioned. If it seems desirable, it is a simple matter to keep count of the number of pieces added and discarded. Generally, however, a busy school librarian hardly has time even for this.

The checked subject heading list will indicate quickly whether a certain subject is in the file. The use of the information file will be greatly facilitated, however, if a see reference card of a different color from that used for books is placed in the card catalog for at least the more important subjects (Figure 19).

```
   WEATHER

      See also material in vertical file under
above subject
```

FIGURE 19
Catalog card for non-book materials

Picture Collection

Pictures are gathered from many sources, largely magazines not being retained for reference purposes. They may be purchased from commercial dealers in pictures, two of whom were mentioned in Chapter 1. Often sets of pictures are listed among free and inexpensive materials in library and educational periodicals. Some good pictorial material is available as publicity from various industries and government agencies.

Mounts for pictures should be of a good variety of tag board secured from any reliable office supply dealer. They should be ordered cut to a uniform size, 10" by 14" being suggested for a legal size file. It is not advisable to mount pictures on various sizes of tag board.

The source of pictures is relatively unimportant, but any title or explanation should be retained. Each picture should be neatly clipped and pasted on a mount in the position which sets it off to advantage. Margins in the ratio of 1 to 2, top and bottom, with equal margins on the two sides furnish very good proportions. Several small pictures on the same subject are better grouped on one mount than shown singly on individual mounts. The first small picture on a given subject might well be pasted in the upper left-hand corner of the mount in the expectation that others will be found to complete the group. All mounts should be filed with the long side down in the file and the subject headings should be lettered along the upper right-hand edge. This is obviously more convenient for most readers who will be moving mounts with the right hand and will read subject headings simultaneously. A good list for subject headings is the *Picture File in School, College and Public Libraries.*[4] The school library stamp should be placed on the back of each mount.

School librarians should consult teachers regarding the types of pictures that will be useful for classroom work. It is suggested that loose pictures be kept in large envelopes, the same size as the mounts, and with subject heading in the upper right-hand corner.

[4] Norma Olin Ireland, *Picture File in School, College and Public Libraries*, rev. and enl. ed. (Boston: F. W. Faxon Company, 1952)

These envelopes may be bought or made of heavy brown paper, folded to size with generous flaps on all four sides to hold the pictures inside. They should be filed just in front of mounted pictures bearing the same subject heading. When mounted pictures on a given subject are out or do not seem to meet the need of the moment, teachers and older pupils may be allowed to look through the loose ,pictures and select others more suitable to be mounted. In this way, the library builds a collection of pictures that meet school needs.

A few large plastic folders, secured from any library supply house, may be kept at hand and used to circulate valuable pictures or those with full descriptions on the back of the pictures which would be lost to view were they pasted on a mount. These plastic folders should be removed when pictures are returned to the files, since they are intended only for protection while pictures are in use in the classrooms.

Audio-Visual Materials

The preparation of audio-visual materials is largely a question of housing. It is here advised that audio-visual materials should not be housed on open shelves with other materials, although this is sometimes suggested for school libraries. To begin with, the nature and content of these materials cannot be learned from mere handling. They need instead to be viewed. Furthermore, they should be handled as little as possible and always with greatest care. Another reason for housing audio-visual materials elsewhere than in the reading room is that they need shelves, drawers, etc., especially designed for their use; and they also need to be housed where the temperature and humidity can be controlled to some extent. Schools which have considerable collections of such materials are advised to house them in a room planned especially for the purpose. In schools with limited holdings, the audio-visual materials may be housed in the librarian's office, workroom, or storage space where their handling can be more closely supervised. *Audio-Visual School Library Service* by Margaret Rufsvold, though now somewhat out of date, has been cited as the best guide for handling such materials and school librarians are advised to consult this work for details.

There are various types of arrangement used for audio-visual materials. Some librarians classify them by the Dewey Decimal Classification which automatically determines their location on shelves or in drawers as the case may be. Others assign an accession number, as in the case of books, to each piece of audio-visual material as it is received in the library and the item is located on the shelves or in a drawer by the accession number. Still others use a number designating a fixed location on the shelves or in drawers. For instance, 1-3-26 would mean that the material belongs in section one, shelf three, in position 26.

Since teachers and pupils usually seek all materials by subjects, many school librarians advocate placing at least a subject card in the card catalog for each item of audio-visual material. A card of a different color from that used to designate books and material in the vertical file should be used. This card will indicate where the desired item may be located whether arrangement is by the Dewey Decimal system, accession number, or by a combination of numbers indicating fixed location in a drawer or on a shelf. A separate shelf list should be maintained for audio-visual materials, since they will not be shelved with the books.

Whatever designating number is used, it may be placed on the label of films or filmstrips, or lettered on adhesive tape attached to the side of the container. In the case of recordings, the number could be lettered on an album of recordings or on each separate record.

Films may be provided with charging equipment in a manner similar to that suggested for books. The pocket, book card, and date-due slip may all be attached to the inside of the top of the container which holds each film. Charging equipment may also be attached to albums of recordings or to separate records not arranged in albums. Filmstrips present more of a problem since their containers are too small to allow space for charging equipment. In Chapter 3 there is a discussion of the circulation of materials which are not supplied with charging equipment.

Conclusion

Materials carefully prepared, in order on shelves and in files, greatly enhance the use of the library and simplify the work of the school librarian and his assistants. They also give satisfaction to students and teachers who turn to the library for all types of materials when they are needed and are impatient when it seems that lack of order and unnecessary red tape prevent materials from being readily available. Circulation routines, discussed in the following chapter, are set up on the assumption that well-prepared materials are available in an orderly arrangement.

CHAPTER 3

CIRCULATION OF MATERIALS

Introduction

Circulation work is the backbone of library service. The circulation desk is usually the first contact which readers have with the library and for many readers remains their chief contact. This is true in a school library no less than in others because to many pupils, the library is largely the place "to check out a book."

Since the school librarian needs to give time during the school day almost exclusively to reference work, reading guidance, and other types of service for pupils and teachers, the care of the circulation desk must be left largely to pupil assistants. The librarian will, to be sure, supervise circulation work at all times, advising and answering questions as they arise. There will also be times when he will take a turn at the circulation desk, if only because pupils are not available. This is a desirable practice since work at the circulation desk gives the librarian an excellent opportunity to know what books are popular with boys and girls and what units of study are in progress in various classrooms. Work at the circulation desk also shows the librarian what demands the library fails to meet—demands that may well be reflected in future book orders. The librarian will find it helpful, too, to look over the cards being filed in the circulation file after the day's work is done.

Pupil Assistants

Pupil assistants assigned to the circulation desk should be chosen with special care. Their scholarship records should insure that they can easily learn and keep in mind the multitudinous desk routines, as well as justify their taking time from studies to devote to library work. They should be thoroughly familiar with the location of all materials in the school library. They should themselves be interested in reading and discussing books if they are to assist in simple reading guidance of fellow pupils. It is most important that they should have sufficient self-discipline so that the librarian will not have to tell them more than once that they are not to study while on desk duty and not to talk to other pupils except about library matters. It is most important that they should have mature judgment sufficient to decide when to go ahead on their own and when the librarian should be consulted. Since much practice in the preparation of materials, and in shelving, mending, etc. should precede work at the loan desk, it follows that circulation of materials in the school library will in all probability be performed by the older, more mature and experienced pupil assistants. This plan of procedure will furthermore give pupil assistants in training a goal toward which to strive, because they usually prefer circulation duties to other types of library work. A full discussion of the use of pupil assistants will be found in Mary Peacock Douglas's *The Pupil Assistant in the School Library* (American Library Association, 1957).

Library Policy

Before circulation routines are established, a policy must be formed as to which materials should circulate and for what lengths of time, and whether they should circulate to both pupils and teachers. There is also the matter of overdues and fines, involving such questions as: When a book is overdue, how much time should be allowed to lapse before overdue notices are sent to the reader? Shall the library charge fines and, if so, should the same amount be charged for non-book materials as for books? When a book is lost, how much should the reader be required to pay?

A survey of any group of school librarians would prove that they vary as to policy in these as in other phases of circulation work. In this chapter, there is suggested a general circulation policy which may be modified to suit the needs of individual libraries which vary as do the schools of which they are a part. A reasonable routine for circulating materials of various kinds is also suggested. Once again, this is not the only possible routine, and it may be modified to suit local conditions. For example, it is not anticipated that all libraries will circulate every type of material. The routine suggested, however, is deemed suitable and practical for those libraries which do circulate both books and other materials. In a few instances, several equally good methods of doing the same thing are suggested, with the understanding that the librarian will adopt that which best suits the needs of his library. The method of filing cards in the circulation tray, discussed later in the chapter, is one instance of these alternating methods.

It *is* strongly advised that a routine for each type of material in the school library be clearly worked out, taught to all who assist in the library, and typed in manual form for consultation when the pupil assistant is doubtful. (For details on the circulation manual see p. 145.) This routine should be followed always in the same manner regardless of the period of the day, who is working at the desk, or who wants to borrow materials. Nothing is more disconcerting than to find an odd assortment of notes stuck here and there on the desk: "Mr. Smith sent Bill to borrow the latest *Scientific Monthly* for his class." "Miss Jones took v. 15 of the *World Book*. Will return at end of period." "Alice Major needs *Little Women* for a book report. Did not sign card but will return after school." A well systematized circulation routine should record every transaction in a uniform manner and show where any desired material may be found.

Book Cards

Every book in the circulating collection should have a book card in its book pocket, both made out in the form suggested in Chapter 2. The book cards for regular books, circulating for two weeks, will be white in color. When books are placed on reserve for use only in the library during the school day and for circulation only overnight, the white card will be replaced by a blue one. The routine for handling reserves will be discussed more fully later in the chapter.

The type of book card that is ruled with spaces for the borrower's signature and homeroom number should be used in a school library. The homeroom number is helpful when the library needs to locate the pupil for any reason. (The pupil's signature is the best possible evidence that he borrowed a certain book from the library.) Though one reader might be tempted to sign the name of another on the card, it is hardly possible that he could successfully imitate the signature. It is not good policy to allow one pupil to sign for another, even with permission, because of resulting complications. - In case this is allowed, the pupil signing should be required to add his own name in parentheses after the name of the borrower for whom he is acting.

Circulation of Reference Books

Books such as encyclopedias and other materials regularly used for reference are usually not provided with book cards and pockets since they do not circulate in the ordinary way. No school library should consider lending reference books for home use. There is wide variation, however, in policy regarding the special circulation of reference materials to classrooms where teachers like to have all types of materials for use with pupils. In the case of materials that do circulate, special classroom collections may be borrowed from the school library for the duration of the unit being studied, as discussed later in the chapter.

There is a good case, however, for not circulating reference materials outside the library. Most of the demand for such materials is made by pupils going to the school library from classrooms or study halls, or from classes brought to the library by their teachers. If reference books are out in classrooms, obviously they cannot be available for use in the library. There is not a great deal of time in the average classroom for the use of reference materials, and teachers can send a student to consult a reference book when class procedure requires it. Finally, the possibility of loss is increased when reference books circulate to classrooms.

A middle-of-the-road policy in this matter might be to mark all reference books with "R" before or above the classification number and omit the book card and pocket, thus designating the books for use in the library only. Materials so marked would be circulated to the classroom only on written request from the teacher, with permission of the librarian, and with the understanding that they must be returned at the end of the period.

In the case of encyclopedias, of which school libraries are strongly urged to purchase a new edition at least every five years, it might be feasible to furnish each volume of the older edition with a pocket and card for extended loan to classrooms. Both teachers and pupils, however, should understand that the new edition, for use only in the library, will contain the most recent information on current topics and should also be consulted.

Some school libraries have found it practical to have one copy of certain titles marked for and kept in the reference collection for use in the library only, while another copy may be placed on the shelves with regular books for circulation. Emily Post's *Etiquette* is one example of a title which might be in both collections, always available to all students doing reference work yet available for circulation when needed for a unit in the home economics classroom, or when a pupil wants to take it for home use.

Any school librarian is also justified in stamping "Not to Circulate" on certain books which, though not in reference, are still in constant demand in the library, even though such books are furnished with pockets and cards. These are convenient for special circulation to a teacher for one-period use in the classroom, for instance, or for general circulation in case the noncirculation status of the book is later changed. An attractive edition of the complete *Mother Goose* with outstanding illustrations or an out-of-print book on costumes might be examples of this type. The accessibility of the book to the largest number of readers is always the prime consideration in circulating materials in a school library.

Equipment for Circulation Work

In a standard circulation desk, obtainable from library supply houses, there will be found trays for holding book cards while the books are circulating. These trays are placed at the front of the desk for easy observation and handling. They are usually spoken of as "sunken trays" because they are placed below the level of the desk with a roller top arrangement for protection when trays are not in use. A smaller type of desk is usually equipped with circulation trays arranged in an upper desk drawer. In case the desk being used for circulation does not have circulation trays, they may be purchased from a library supply house as a separate item and placed either in a drawer or on top of the desk itself. It is recommended that double trays, rather than single ones, be purchased because they are more economical and more useful. The circulation desk should also be equipped with at least one drawer with lock and key for fine money and other things requiring protection.

Guide cards for the days of the month and for special sections, such as "Overdues," will be needed for use in the circulation trays. A stamp should be available for each length of loan to prevent errors caused by changing dates on the stamps for varying periods as the materials are being circulated. Stamps needed for circulation procedures suggested in this chapter will be: 2 weeks, 7 days, 3 days for short-time loans, and the current date for reserved books and materials loaned to teachers. Libraries preferring to circulate materials for only one week and not using short-time loans would need only a stamp each for a 7-day period and the current date. The band dater type of stamp is recommended rather than one in which type must be set by hand. Setting type is time-consuming and the tiny letters and dates are easily misplaced or lost.

Each stamp should be plainly differentiated to avoid confusion in use. This may be easily accomplished by choosing daters with differently colored handles for the different types of loan. Or a piece of adhesive tape may be placed across the flat side of the handle, which designates the front of the stamp, and the length of loan lettered on the tape. It is advisable also to use one color of ink for the current date and another color of ink for all other dates. The stamp which carries the year, as well as the month and day, is helpful when a book is considered for withdrawal because it shows the last date on which the book circulated. Library supply houses carry a small stamp with full date which does not consume undue space.

All stamps should be set before the school opens each morning to avoid confusion of dates in circulation. Some school librarians make a practice of setting the date stamps before closing the library each day. Stamps may even be changed at the beginning of the last period so that cards may be counted and filed before school closes. In any event, it is important that the correct stamps be ready for use when the first reader appears at the desk each morning.

Circulation File

The record kept at the circulation desk by all school libraries is the time record or circulation file. Other types of records which may be kept are the book record, filed by call number, indicating all books that are in circulation and where they may be located, and the readers' record consisting of a card for each reader, arranged alphabetically, on which the record of each charge to a reader is made. Many busy school librarians find the readers' record time-consuming beyond its usefulness. However, a routine for keeping a readers' record will be discussed later in the chapter since many school libraries maintain one. School libraries usually do not attempt to maintain a book record.

Circulation of Regular Books

Regular books are those equipped with white book cards, circulated for a period of two weeks. When a book is brought to the desk for circulation, the reader is asked to remove the card from the book pocket and write his name and homeroom number on the first vacant line. The assistant then stamps the date due on the book card beside the reader's name and on the first vacant space on the date-due slip. The card is held with others for count and filing at the end of the day.

All cards may be held at the front of the circulation tray or behind the guide card for date due of regular books. In either place, book cards should be arranged at least roughly by call number or by whatever other method of filing the library uses, in case it is necessary to consult the cards during the day.

Short-Time Loans

Sometimes the demand on certain titles in the school library makes it necessary to restrict temporarily the time of loan. Examples of such times might well be when a teacher assigns a particular title to be read by the entire class in a limited time, or when a movie is in town and many pupils want to read the book on which the movie is based. It therefore becomes important that as many readers as possible have access to such material within a stated period. The short-time loan seems the best answer when there is real demand for such service.

A very simple method of restricting the period of loan to a brief time is to use a small card marked "3-day" and clip it to the top of the book card of any book being so restricted. It may be well also for the reader's information, and for identification of the book without the book card, to pencil "3-day" lightly on the pocket, to be erased when the 3-day card is removed, after the need for restriction of period of loan has passed. It is further suggested that all books on short-time loans be shelved together in a specially designated place while the demand is great, so that readers may find them quickly without asking.

The only difference in the routine for circulating a book on short-time loan is that the assistant must be sure to use the stamp set for three days. The assistant should also remind the reader that the book is on short-time loan, must be returned after three days and that there can be no renewal. It is reasonable to charge a higher fine on short-time loans than on regular books.

Discharging a Book

The procedure discussed above is known in library work as charging a book, though pupils consistently speak of it as "checking out" a book. The procedure of getting a book that has been circulating back into the library is known as discharging a book, or familiarly as "checking it in."

Regardless of the length of loan, the procedure is the same when a book is returned. The assistant looks at the date due on the date-due slip and informs the reader, in case he is still present, if the book is overdue and how much he owes. It is important to collect the fine at the time of return, if possible, so that no record need be made of the overdue and resulting fine. A routine for handling overdues and fines will be discussed later in the chapter.

From the date due, the assistant finds the card under the corresponding date in the circulation file and returns the book card to the pocket, at the same time checking to see if the accession number is the same as that on the book pocket. If not, the assistant will realize that he has the wrong book card. Many problems in circulation arise ırom getting the wrong card in a book, thus confusing the records of two books and two readers. Every assistant must be urged to make sure that accession numbers match *each* time the book card is returned to the pocket.

The assistant then takes a quick look through the book for damages acquired since the book circulated to the reader. If this is done faithfully and carefully each time a book is returned to the desk, the problem of fixing blame for major damages will be greatly simplified.

The book is then placed with those to be shelved, mended, or rebound. Books ready for the shelves might well be kept on a book truck or section of shelves near the circulation desk where readers may look them over for popular favorites. When readers select recently returned books for circulation, it saves the task of shelving them and also gives the reader a feeling of satisfaction over securing a book that others are reading. The regulation that a book must be replaced on the shelves before circulating again has no place in any school library. Librarians are advised, however, against the practice of allowing readers to crowd around the circulation desk waiting for a recently returned book to be checked in.

Readers' Cards

If readers' cards are used in the school library, the process of charging and discharging a book will be somewhat longer. For this reason, many school librarians feel that there is not time for the readers' record. Some advantages, however, result from the use of the reader's card. Th library then has a complete record of materials borrowed from the library by each pupil. This may eventually become part of the file kept in the school office for each pupil. Readers themselves like to have the cards as they become filled if they are not kept by the school. The reader's card gives the teacher or librarian some idea of the pupil's reading interests. It often answers in part the question of whether a pupil has actually read a book on which he reported. Lastly, the reader's card furnishes an excellent place to record overdues and fines. In fact, this feature alone would seem to justify use of the reader's card.

Readers' cards may be purchased from a library supply house or mimeographed by the school. At the beginning of the school year, a card is filled out for each pupil on the official school roll. These cards should be arranged alphabetically and kept in a separate file at the circulation desk. Cards for new pupils may be added as they enroll in school and cards for pupils who have left school removed so that the file is kept up to date. Going through the file at any time will quickly indicate which pupils have not borrowed materials from the school library, which ones are making only limited use of its resources, and which ones are reading widely.

It is helpful to enter in pencil in the upper right-hand corner of the reader's card the number of each period for which the high school pupil is scheduled in study hall and, if the school has more than one study hall, some indication as to which study hall. If the school has the system by which pupils change homerooms each semester, the homeroom on the card may be lettered in pencil as well. Information as to the homeroom and study hall is helpful when the library needs to reach the pupil for any reason. This record may also show in code the reading level of each student, a great help in reading guidance, especially on the elementary level (Figure 20). It is essential that the school library maintain an alphabetical file of all pupils for reasons indicated above. The use of this file as a readers' record is optional, though the routine for keeping the readers' record is outlined here.

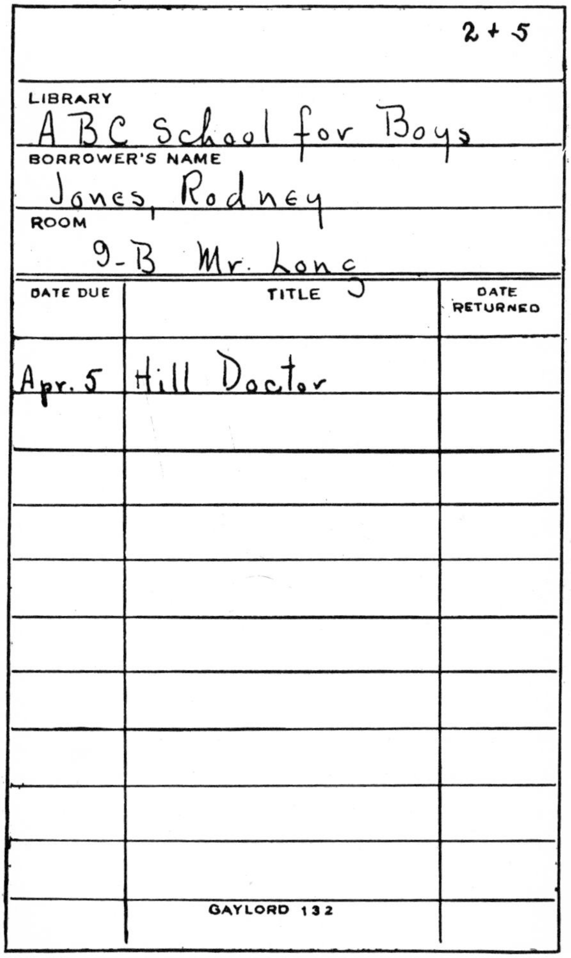
2 + 5

LIBRARY
ABC School for Boys

BORROWER'S NAME
Jones, Rodney

ROOM
9-B Mr. Long

DATE DUE	TITLE	DATE RETURNED
Apr. 5	Hill Doctor	

GAYLORD 132

FIGURE 20
Reader's card

Use of the Reader's Card

In charging out a book, after the reader has signed his name and homeroom number on the book card, the assistant identifies the name and draws the corresponding card from the readers' file. While the assistant is stamping the date due on the book card and date-due slip, the reader is asked to write the brief title of the book on his own reader's card. In the case of very small children, the assistant will have to write the title. The assistant then adds the date due beside the title on the reader's card before it is returned to the file. Time may be saved at the desk by having the assistant make the record on the reader's card after the reader has taken the book. However, there is some advantage in handling the reader's card while he is present.

The handling of the reader's card furnishes an opportunity for the pupil to note, or for his attention to be called to, any overdues or fines charged to him. Often this reminder is sufficient to cause the reader to return the overdue book or pay the fine and receive credit on his reader's card. Sometimes the assistant, with the aid of the reader, is able to clear up errors that have been made at the desk.

The reader's card is also used when a book is returned to the desk. From the name on the book card, the assistant draws the corresponding reader's card from the file and stamps the date returned, using the stamp for current date, on the card. Any fine which should be charged is noted in the space marked "Date returned" (Figure 20). If the reader is still present, he is reminded of the fine and given credit for any amount paid. A fine notice should be prepared and the card "flagged" with a colored signal when the amount of fines owed reaches a stated sum.

Any form of reader's card which must be presented by the reader for each transaction at the desk is not recommended in a school library. There are chances for too many complications caused by the reader's failure to have his card with him when he wishes to take a book from the library.

Record of reserved books borrowed for overnight use is not made on the reader's card. This applies as well to all materials used in the school for only part of the school day. The record of materials other than books on the reader's card will be discussed later in the chapter.

Renewals

Some school libraries solve the problem of renewals by not allowing any. The theory behind this policy is that, if a pupil has not finished reading a book within the two-week period of regular loan, it is not likely that he will do so. The privilege of renewal may encourage some pupils to delay the reading of a book from the school library. There are occasions, however, when a rush of duties prevents even the best reader from completing a book in which he is intensely interested, or which he needs for a class assignment, before the end of the two-week loan. Renewal is a library service which he greatly appreciates. It is suggested that renewal of one week be granted on all regular loans of two weeks. Some libraries may prefer renewals of two weeks so that the date due will be the same as that for a regular loan. At the same time, it is urged that pupils be taught to use the privilege of renewal only when it is necessary to complete a book. It will help in identifying 7-day cards when count is being made if a paper clip is placed on each card of a book renewed. The clip will be removed before each card is filed.

It is strongly recommended that renewals be charged only with the book present. This practice is no hardship in school libraries to which each reader has daily access. It will prevent a request for renewal when a pupil has neglected to return the book and wishes to avoid paying a fine. Besides, presenting the book for renewal is the best possible evidence that the book is not missing.

A book is renewed in almost the identical manner in which it was charged out in the first place, after the corresponding book card has been located in the date-due file. It is suggested, however, that "R" placed under the reader's signature and beside the date due for the renewal on the book card will save the reader's having to repeat his name and homeroom.

As implied earlier, the privilege of renewal should apply only to regular two-week books; otherwise, the briefer periods of loan lose their significance.

New Cards

Whenever the circulation assistant notices that the last line of a book card has been used for the reader's signature, he should tear the card on the left side half-way across to call attention to the fact that a new card is needed. When the book is returned to the desk, and the book card with the tear across is returned to the book pocket, the book should be laid aside with others awaiting repairs so that a new card may be made.

If, however, a reader finds that there is no space left on the book card for his signature, the assistant should supply a new book card on which the reader signs his name and homeroom number. The new card with date due stamped on it is then clipped to the original card and held until there is time to make a new card. It is suggested that the two cards, clipped together, not be placed in the circulation file because of the possibility of their becoming separated and therefore meaningless.

Whenever a new card is made, "cd. 2" should be typed, preferably in red, at the center top of the card. This will help calculate the approximate number of circulations of the book when it is considered for replacement or withdrawal. The filled-up book card should be destroyed since it is no longer useful.

Snags

A "snag" is caused in circulation when the book card for a given book is apparently missing after the book has been returned to the desk. A good routine for handling a snag is to look first for the card under date due. If it is not found, search should be made through cards for the day before and for the day after date due. Often the missing card has somehow got into either of these two files. In case the card still cannot be found, the book should be placed under the desk with other books thus designated as snags. As time permits, the entire circulation file should be searched and, if the book card is not found, the book should be laid aside for a new card to be made. This card should have typed in red at the center top "Dup. cd." as distinguished from a "2d cd." mentioned earlier. In case the original card should later appear, the card which is more nearly filled up may be destroyed.

Ordinarily, books with missing cards should not be allowed to circulate. However, in case it is necessary for the book to be used during the time the book is a snag, certainly for classroom use, a book card may be filled out in pencil, thus indicating a temporary card, on which the book may circulate. The temporary card should be made a duplicate card as outlined above, when the book is returned and the original card is still missing.

Reserves

There are two types of reserves, those requested by teachers for the use of their classes and those which readers reserve for personal use. They are generally known respectively as "teacher reserves" or "class reserves" and "personal reserves" or "reader reserves." Many school libraries do not allow personal reserves, maintaining with reason that the process is time-consuming and that readers, with daily access to the school library, can easily watch out for any highly desired book. Also, while any book is being held for one reader, it is not available to many other readers who may need to use it. However, the privilege of reserving a book is appreciated by readers and a simple routine is suggested below for use in libraries permitting personal reserves.

Reader Reserves

To reduce the number of personal or reader reserves, the privilege may be restricted to certain books. Some school libraries will reserve a book for a pupil only if it is needed definitely for a class assignment. The privilege of personal reserves should not be extended to books that are on reserve for class use, or to books already on short-time loan.

When a reader asks that a book be reserved, he should be given a card for the purpose on which he signs his name and homeroom number, after the card has been filled out (Figure 21a). The card must have all information—call number, author, and brief title—necessary to find the book card in the circulation file and the reader should supply this. To make sure the desired book is not in the library, the assistant should check the shelves before reserving a book. The date on which the reserve is requested should be stamped on the card.

The assistant then searches in the circulation file for the book card for the desired title. The reserve card is then folded and attached with a paper clip to the book card, thus calling attention to the fact that there is a reserve on the book. If there are several reserves for the same book, and the shelf list indicates more than one copy, it is wise to find other cards for this title in the circulation file, rather than clipping all reserves to the same book card. To help solve the problem of the reader's getting the book in the order of his request, each succeeding request should be clipped on the book card next due in the circulation file, though it is true that no one can predict that books will be returned in the order of date due.

When the book is returned and the clipped book card is placed in the book, it should be shelved under the desk with other books reserved for readers. The reserve card should be filled out as in Figure 21b. A notice is made out and sent to the reader who first requested the book, as indicated by the date stamped on the reserve card (Figure 22).

Usually a period of three days is allowed for the reader to receive the notice and report to the library for the book. The 3-day stamp should be used on the notice sent to the reader, showing the length of time that the book will be held. If after three days the book has not been called for, notice should be sent to the next reader reserving it. In case there is not another reserve, the book is shelved with others for regular circulation. The reserve card should be kept for use again until the four spaces are filled.

Class Reserves

When any class is working on a certain topic, a period of history, for example, or some other project, the teacher usually

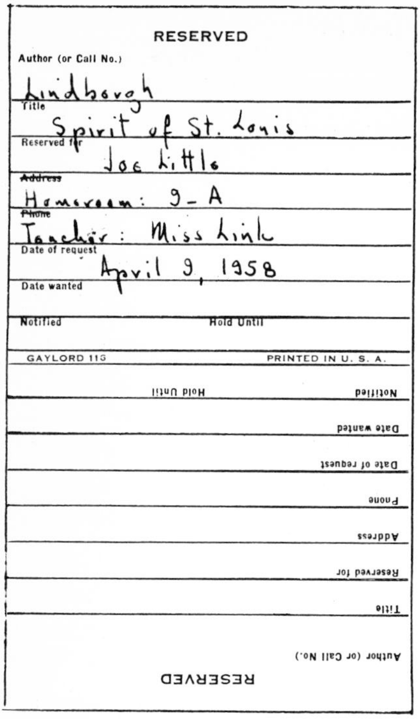
RESERVED

Author (or Call No.)
Lindbergh
Title
Spirit of St. Louis
Reserved for
Joe Little
~~Address~~
Homeroom: 9 - A
~~Phone~~
Teacher: Miss Link
Date of request
April 9, 1958
Date wanted

Notified Hold Until

GAYLORD 116 PRINTED IN U. S. A.

FIGURE 21a
Book reserved by reader

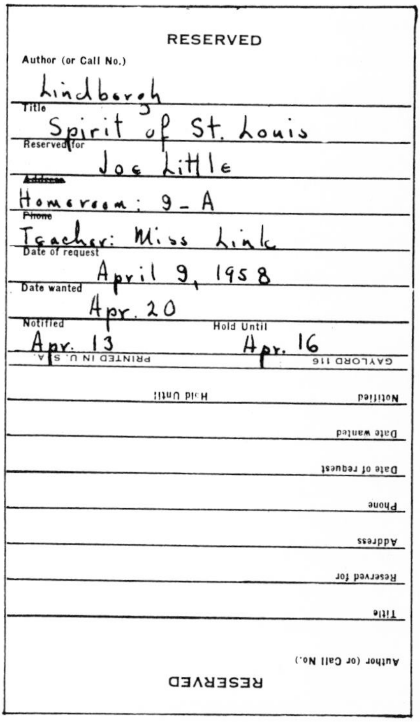
RESERVED

Author (or Call No.)
Lindbergh
Title
Spirit of St. Louis
Reserved for
Joe Little
~~Address~~
Homeroom: 9 - A
~~Phone~~
Teacher: Miss Link
Date of request
April 9, 1958
Date wanted
Apr. 20
Notified Hold Until
Apr. 13 Apr. 16

FIGURE 21b
Card filled out when book returns

```
┌──────────────────────────────────────────────────────────────┐
│                     LIBRARY NOTICE                             │
│   Room   9_ A _ Miss Link                                      │
│   Name   Joe Little                      Date Apr. 13, 1958    │
│                                                                │
│      Please come to the library to see about the following:    │
│      Spirit of St. Louis, by Lindbergh.                        │
│   _____  │
│                                                                │
│   _____  │
│                                                                │
│      ☐  Now ready for your use.                                │
│      ☐  Now needed in the library.                             │
│      ☑  Reserved by you but not called for.                    │
│      ☐  Now overdue.                                           │
│      ☐  On which there is a fine of_____             │
│                                                                │
│   PRINTED IN U.S.A.          Mary Smith            Librarian   │
└──────────────────────────────────────────────────────────────┘
```

FIGURE 22

Notice of reserve book sent to reader

requests that certain materials be put on reserve for use by students in the library during the school day and for use at home overnight. While reader reserves may be optional, every high school library and some elementary libraries will undoubtedly be called upon to arrange class reserves.

It is wise to have a regular form for each teacher to fill out when requesting books to be reserved (Figure 23). Reserving books should be discouraged until the form has been filled out and submitted to the librarian. This caution is given to prevent the tendency on the part of some teachers to have books put on reserve by oral request. Using a request form is about the only way to keep an accurate record of what is on reserve and when the books should be removed from the reserved shelves. Unless teachers request that books be placed on reserve before a class assignment is made requiring their use, the librarian will probably learn that books should be on reserve only because of constant demand. The problem becomes more acute after such books have been charged out to the more eager pupils and must be recalled to be put on reserve. Teachers should be encouraged as far as possible to reserve all books for a group at one time, instead of

Request for Classroom Reserves in the School Library

Please place the following books on reserve for use by my classes in American History from

_____ to _____

Signed _____, Teacher

Call number	Author	Title

FIGURE 23

Form for request for books to be placed on reserve

adding to their reserves a few books at a time without proper records at the desk.

The routine for handling class reserves is fairly simple. When the request form for reserves arrives from the teacher, a pupil assistant looks up the call number of each book desired, places it in the space provided on the form and secures the books from the shelves. In case some of the books requested for reserve are in circulation, efforts should be made to have them returned promptly.

The white card is removed from the book pocket and marked "Reserved," with the name of the class for which it is reserved or by the name of the teacher requesting that the book be placed on reserve. Whatever is used (the name of the teacher, the class for which the book is reserved, or both) to mark the shelf where this reserved book is to be shelved should appear on the white card. The current date is stamped beside the word "Reserved" on the book card, indicating when the book has been placed on reserve. While the book is on reserve, the white book card is filed with cards for other books on reserve following whatever form of filing is used in the circulation file.

A blue card, duplicating the white one, is made out and placed in the book for use in circulation. For prompt shelving and to indicate that the book is on reserve when the book card is not in the book, an overnight card is also placed in the book pocket to remain there even when the book is circulating. It is helpful for shelving to enter on the overnight card the name of the class for which the book is reserved, the teacher who requested that the book be put on reserve, or both according to the library policy for marking reserve shelves (Figure 24). These overnight cards may be ordered from a library supply house or cut to size in the library and typed as needed. Advantages of making the cards are that the overnight card may be the same color as the reserve book card and cut long enough to protrude beyond the top of the book so that, wherever the book is seen, it will be designated as being on reserve. No record of circulation is made on these overnight cards so they last for a long time. When any book is taken off reserve, both cards are removed and kept on file until

```
OVERNIGHT
BOOK
——
To be returned before the
first class the following
school day.

American History
Miss Manley




GAYLORD 140
```

FIGURE 24
Overnight card for reserved book

needed again. The white book card is returned to the book pocket and the book is shelved again with others for regular circulation.

All books on reserve at any time should be shelved near the circulation desk for supervision by pupil assistants on duty. The average school library allows pupils to use books from the reserved shelves without getting permission or having to sign for them during the school day. However, in larger schools or in schools where the demand for reserves is heavy or there is tendency for the books to get out of the library without benefit of charging, it becomes necessary to ask each pupil to sign at the desk for each circulation in the library.

Reserved books may usually be borrowed after school or during the last period for home use overnight. The pupil signs his name and homeroom number on the blue book card and the assistant stamps the current date on the book card and the date-due slip. Because the blue cards must be handled again the following morning, they should not be made a part of the circulation file but kept at the front of the circulation tray after the count is made.

Reserved books must be returned by a specified time the following morning, usually at least by the end of the half hour after school opens. There is also ordinarily a higher fine on them. Reserved books should be placed on the reserved shelves as soon as possible after they are returned to the library so that pupils using the library the first period of the day may have access to them.

Homeroom Representatives

It may prove helpful to have a representative from each homeroom assigned to work with the library. These pupils may take turns at the job, each for a month at a time, or the teacher may prefer that one interested and reliable pupil keep it for a semester. Among the duties assigned to the homeroom representative is that of collecting all books, including those on reserve, due in the library and returning them during the first half-hour period each morning, assuming that this is the homeroom period. This cuts down traffic in the halls and also reduces the number of books that become misplaced in, or lost from, classrooms before the pupils can go to the library to return them. The homeroom representative may also take notices of fines, overdues and reader reserves to pupils of his homeroom, thus saving time and energy in locating each pupil. As soon as reserved books are checked in each morning, the remaining cards for books not yet returned should be consulted for names and homeroom numbers and an effort made by a pupil assistant to retrieve the missing books.

Non-Book Materials

Materials other than books pose a problem in circulation because it is ordinarily not practical to provide non-book materials with book cards and pockets. However, unless a satisfactory routine is worked out for the occasional circulation of such materials, the desk will find itself cluttered up with a number of informal records, all improvised on the spur of the moment.

The librarian must of necessity first establish a policy regarding the circulation of non-book materials and covering the following questions: Which materials will be circulated? For what period of loan? For use in school only or for home use as well? To pupils and teachers alike? School libraries vary as to policy regarding these and other problems in circulating non-book materials. On the assumption that they are to be circulated, a simple routine is suggested for each type of non-book material.

Magazines

There are arguments against circulating magazines and a school library is justified in not allowing them to circulate. If magazines are to be used for reference purposes, they must be available at all times. The loss, of course, is greater when magazines circulate, especially for home use, and the library is faced with having to expend time and money to replace missing issues, if indeed they can be replaced. Also magazines in circulation are subject to a greater degree of damage than when used only in the library. On the other hand, circulation of magazines increases their total use and is a help to the student working on a paper or project which cannot be done entirely in the library.

In the discussion regarding the preparation of magazines for use in Chapter 2, it was suggested that "Do Not Circulate" be stamped in the upper left-hand corner of the back cover of each magazine issue. When the next current issue arrives and is stamped as suggested above, a small slip of paper should be pasted over the stamp on the back cover of the previous issue, thus signifying that it is no longer current and may now be circulated. The small slip of paper serves also as a date-due slip for the magazine, since the number of circulations is usually small. It is well to keep in the reading room about three issues of monthly magazines and three to four back issues of weeklies since they will be the ones most likely to circulate. Afterwards they may be placed with other issues of the same title kept for reference purposes in the storage room.

Library supply houses offer a card for the circulation of magazines. A stack of these should be kept on hand in every school library which circulates magazines. At least one card should be made out for each magazine title to be circulated and others made as needed, since more than one card will be needed for titles in heavy demand. Unlike book cards, magazine cards are not made out for any particular issue of the magazine, though they are used only for one magazine title. When not in use for circulation, magazine cards are kept in a special file at the circulation desk arranged alphabetically by the titles of magazines.

When a reader presents one or more issues of a magazine to be circulated, the assistant removes from the above-mentioned file of cards one for each magazine title being borrowed. The reader lists on the card the date of issue of each magazine being taken and signs his name and homeroom below the charge. The assistant checks to make sure the dates of issue on the card correspond to those on the magazines and stamps with the 7-day stamp the date due on each magazine card beside the pupil's name, and also on the small slip of paper pasted on the back cover of the magazine which serves as a date-due slip. The reader should be reminded that magazines will be due back in one week rather than two, as in the case of books. The magazine card should be held with others for count and filing at the end of the day. It will save time if the assistant adds the number of issues being taken on each card and places the total there (Figure 25).

When the magazines are returned, the assistant secures from the circulation file under the title of the magazine the card which corresponds to the issues being returned. If all issues charged on the card have been returned, the card is put back into the file of magazine cards until needed again. The magazines, after being examined for major damages, are placed with other materials to be shelved or mended.

If one or more issues are not returned, a line should be drawn through the dates of issues which have been returned and the magazine card placed back in the circulation file from which it

Scientific American

DATE OF MAGAZINE	BORROWER'S NAME	TIME DUE
Feb. 1958		
Mar. 1958	Allen Hill	Jun. 1, 1958

FIGURE 25
Magazine card with charge

Vertical File
AUTHOR

TITLE

DATE DUE	BORROWER'S NAME	ROOM NUMBER
2	First aid	
1	Costume - American	
	Colonial	
3	Authors - M-R	
Apr. 7	Daisy Beon	9-B Tate

GAYLORD NO. 65

FIGURE 26
Vertical file charge card

was removed to await return of other issues. If the reader is present, he should be asked to return the other issues as soon as possible. If the magazines returned are already overdue, the reader should be notified of any fine and given credit for any amount paid. Otherwise, a fine notice should be prepared to send to his homeroom next morning by the homeroom representative, or delivered to the borrower during study hall period.

Some libraries provide each issue of the magazines to be circulated with a magazine card, made out for that particular issue, a pocket and date-due slip. Others omit the pocket but paste on a date-due slip and attach the magazine card to the back cover of each issue with a paper clip. Neither method is suggested for a school library because it is both expensive and time-consuming to supply each issue with a card, pocket, and date-due slip when the limited circulation of magazines hardly justifies it. Many magazines will not circulate at all and others only once or twice during the period of circulation. The use of a card for each individual issue is justified only when a magazine which tends to disappear must be kept at the desk for circulation in the library during the day.

Information File Material

Because materials from the information or vertical file can so easily become disarranged and lost, it is suggested that only the librarian remove material from the file and replace it after use. Circulation of vertical file materials should be limited as far as possible to use within the library itself. This applies especially to material that cannot be easily replaced. However, since there may be need for some of the materials to be taken to classrooms or circulated for home use, a routine for circulation is suggested for a three-day period. At the same time, it should be emphasized that there is heavy loss of vertical file material which is circulated.

Brown envelopes of various sizes which bring magazines and pamphlets to the library should be kept at the desk for circulating materials from the vertical file. Further equipment consists of a supply of book cards different in color from those used for circulating books. At the top of each card Vertical File should be lettered.

When a reader wishes to borrow material from the vertical file, the assistant takes from the special file on the desk a card marked Vertical File and has the reader list on the card the subject headings of materials being borrowed with the number of pieces on each subject. The pupil then signs his name and homeroom below the charge. The assistant checks the materials with the charge on the card and totals the number of pieces being taken. Then he stamps date due, using the 3-day stamp, on the card beside the pupil's name. From the card the assistant copies the charge on an envelope of the size to fit the largest piece of material being taken, has the reader sign his name and homeroom at the bottom of the charge and stamps date due beside it. Then the assistant draws a circle to enclose the charge and places the material in the envelope. As he does so, the assistant checks the number of pieces on each subject and reminds the reader to return material in the same envelope, using the charge on the envelope to determine what materials should be returned. The reader should be reminded also that material from the vertical file circulates for only three days. The card is held with others for count and filing at the end of the day (Figure 26).

When vertical file material is returned to the desk, the assistant checks the date due, then finds under the date due in the file the card with a charge which corresponds to that on the envelope. If all material has been returned, a line is drawn through the charge on the envelope before it is returned to its place with others at the desk to be used again. The vertical file card is returned to the file of similar cards. The material itself, after examination for damages, is laid aside either with materials to be mended or returned to the file.

If some items have not been brought back in the envelope, those that have been returned are marked off the card which is then replaced in the date-due file until material is returned. Again, if the reader is still present, he is told of any overdues or fines owed and given credit for payment.

It must be emphasized that count is made of the number of pieces of all non-book materials (magazines, vertical file materials, pictures, etc.) rather than the number of cards. For this reason, it is well when the material is charged out for the assistant to add the number of pieces and write it on the card. Then the person making the count at the end of the day will not have to do so. Because the charging of such materials usually consumes considerable space on the card, the assistant must replace cards for non-book materials rather frequently.

Circulation of Pictures

Pictures are used frequently in classrooms for special reports, for displays on subjects being studied, or for posting on the bulletin board. For this reason, the school library will probably be lenient in the number of pictures which may be borrowed at one time. However, for those who might take undue advantage of such leniency, it is suggested that pictures borrowed at any one time be limited to 25 for each reader, with not more than 10 pictures on any one subject. It was suggested in Chapter 2 that only pictures that are mounted be circulated in a school library with provision that loose pictures selected by the reader be mounted on request. Because pictures will be needed for a longer period of time, it is suggested that their period of loan be two weeks, without privilege of renewal.

Pictures may be circulated in exactly the same manner as suggested above for vertical file material. In fact, for schools which have only limited requests for the circulation of pictures, this method is recommended. It would be wise, however, to use a card of still a different color and letter Picture Collection at the top of the card. Where the demand for pictures is heavy, p-slips (3″ by 5″ slips) may be used instead of cards. The routine for circulation of pictures by use of p-slips is outlined for libraries which circulate pictures in quantity.

Pictures may be circulated in large brown envelopes purchased for the purpose, or folders made from heavy brown paper, large enough to hold 10″ by 14″ mounts. The envelopes should be a full inch longer and wider than the mounts to allow room for groups of pictures. On the front of each envelope or folder, which will be used over and over as long as it lasts, should be pasted a date-due slip. In this instance, the slip is pasted down flat so as not to be torn off and lost.

When a reader brings pictures to the desk, the assistant inserts a piece of carbon paper, cut to size, between two p-slips and asks the reader to list the subject headings from the mounts and place beside each the number of pictures being taken on each subject. The reader then signs his name and homeroom below the charge. The assistant letters the reader's name in form for filing at the top of the slip and stamps date due, using the 2-week stamp, beside the reader's name. He also enters the total number of pictures being taken (Figure 27). In the case of very young readers, the assistant will save time by making the entire charge, being sure that the reader signs his name and homeroom. The assistant then stamps the date due on the slip pasted on the folder and has the reader write his name and homeroom beside the date due. This is to help identify the folder, which may become confused with others in the classroom during the time pictures are in use.

As the assistant places the pictures in the folder, he checks to make sure that the reader is taking all pictures listed on the slip. The carbon copy of the slip, on which date due has been stamped, is clipped to the inside fold of the brown folder. The reader is advised to return the pictures in the same folder and to check the number and subjects of the pictures being returned against the record on the slip inside the folder. A rubber band is then placed around the package of pictures enclosed in the folder. The original p-slip is kept for count and filing in the circulation file.

When pictures are returned, the assistant checks date due stamped on the date-due slip pasted on the front of the brown folder, then finds under date due, filed alphabetically by the reader's name, the p-slip on which the charge matches that on the p-slip clipped to the inside of the folder. If all pictures have

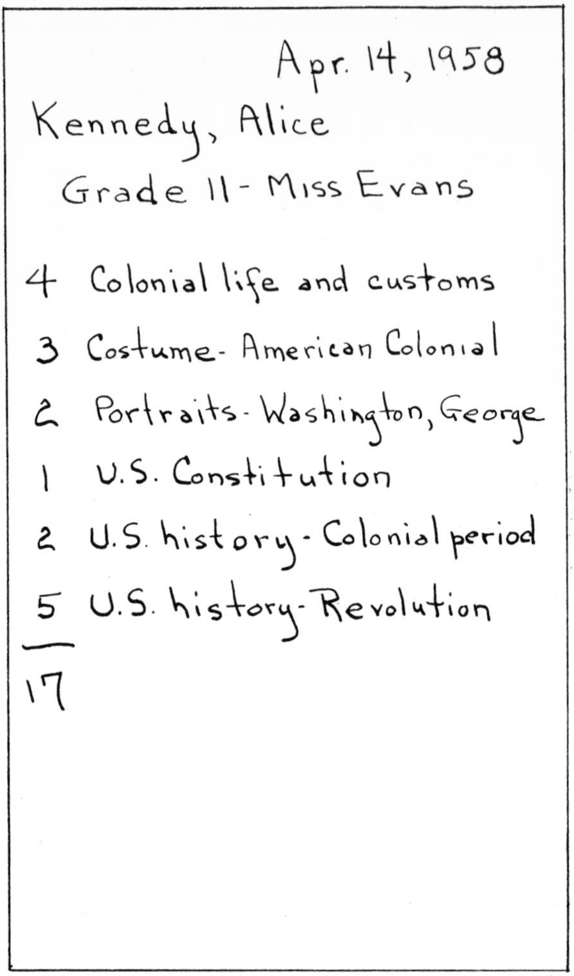

Apr. 14, 1958

Kennedy, Alice

Grade 11 - Miss Evans

4 Colonial life and customs

3 Costume - American Colonial

2 Portraits - Washington, George

1 U.S. Constitution

2 U.S. history - Colonial period

5 U.S. history - Revolution

17

FIGURE 27
Charge slip for pictures

been returned, both p-slips may be destroyed, the folder placed
with others to be used again and the pictures, following examination for damages, placed with other pictures to be repaired or
returned to the picture file.

If, however, some pictures have not been returned, a line
should be drawn through the number returned on the p-slip,
which is then replaced in the circulation file to await return of

missing pictures. The reader should be told which pictures were not returned and asked to look for them. In fact, the amended carbon copy of the p-slip may be given to him as a reminder of missing items. Also, if fines are paid, credit should be given the reader as in other types of circulation. The routine for handling fines will be discussed later in the chapter.

When charging non-book materials on the reader's card, if the school library favors keeping a readers' record, it is suggested that only the total number of magazines, pieces of material from the vertical file, or mounted pictures be entered on the card so that the charge will occupy only one line.

Audio-Visual Materials

In many school systems, films, filmstrips, and other types of audio-visual materials are provided to schools from a centralized collection where circulation methods are different from those of the individual school library. But every school library will probably own some audio-visual materials which are circulated directly from the library. Or the library may serve as the distribution center, borrowing audio-visual materials from the centralized collection, then lending them to teachers in the school. It is well, therefore, to establish a definite routine for the circulation of audio-visual materials, whether they are the property of the school library or have been borrowed from a centralized collection. Since they are chiefly for classroom use, audio-visual materials are seldom if ever circulated to pupils.

If films, recordings, etc. are fitted with cards, pockets, and date-due slips, as was suggested in Chapter 2 as a possibility, then their method of circulation would follow that recommended for books. Where this is not feasible, audio-visual materials may be circulated in exactly the same manner as that suggested for material from the vertical file. It is suggested that a card of a different color from those used for other types of materials be adopted and that Audio-Visual Materials be lettered at the top. The title of each item borrowed should be written on the card and, if it seems wise to designate the type of material represented by each title, F for film, F S for filmstrip, R for recording, etc., might be used after each title—for example, *How to Use the Library* (F S). As in the case of other non-book materials, for ease in counting, the assistant should write on the card the total number of items borrowed on each card. Since audio-visual materials are circulated only to teachers, these cards will be dated with the current date and filed in the special file for teachers as described in the following section.

Where projectors, screens, etc. are housed in the library and are borrowed for one period only, a sign sheet is probably the most practical method of handling the circulation of all audio-visual materials. In fact, many school librarians strongly advise this method for the circulation of audio-visual materials even when equipment is not housed in and circulated from the library. On the sheet for the day, charge is entered for all audio-visual materials and equipment being taken and the teacher signs his name. On return, a line is drawn through the charge. All audio-visual materials should be returned to the library as soon as possible after use.

Materials Circulated to Teachers

Materials borrowed from the school library by teachers may present some problems if they are circulated in the manner suggested for pupils and the cards for teachers' materials are filed in the regular date-due file. The reasons are obvious. Teachers are constantly borrowing from the library large quantities of materials of various kinds which circulate for different periods of loan. They return certain materials at the end of the school day, others after a few days, but they may keep some for extended periods of time. Then too a teacher borrows some materials for his personal use but much more for use in the classroom while pupils are working on a unit of study. It is also difficult to inform a teacher what materials are charged out to him at any time if cards of various charges are scattered throughout the circulation file.

A fairly simple solution is to have a special file for charges to teachers, this file consisting of a series of guide cards, each lettered with the name of a teacher, arranged in alphabetical order. Materials are charged to teachers in accordance with the routines suggested above except that the teacher does not add homeroom after his name and the date stamped on the card and date-due slip is always the date on which the material was taken out. This date shows how long the teacher has had certain materials when they are requested for use elsewhere in the school. It would seem reasonable to recall any requested material that has been charged out to a teacher for at last two weeks, though any period is hard to determine arbitrarily. Because the charge will not bear date due, fines will never be charged against teachers, nor overdue notices sent to them. There may, to be sure, be a few teachers in almost any school who will abuse the privileges inherent in the above routine for charging materials, but most teachers will appreciate such privileges and make every effort to return materials promptly so that others may have access to them.

Cards for materials charged to each teacher, after count has been made, should be filed behind the guide card bearing his name in the same order as that decided upon for filing cards under date due. Teachers may find out quickly what materials are charged to them by consulting charge cards filed behind their own guide cards. At the end of each semester, certainly at the end of each school year, notice should be sent to each teacher listing materials which have not yet been returned. Some school librarians find it helpful to send such notices at the end of each school month or six-week period. This will facilitate the return of materials to the school library and prevent some losses. The routine notice will also help to detect errors when material has been returned to the library but has not been duly recorded.

Classroom Collections

Since classroom collections have been mentioned several times, a further word about them seems appropriate. A classroom collection is a group of books and other materials borrowed by the teacher from the centralized library collection to be used in the classroom while a specific unit of study is in progress. Such

materials supplement pupils' textbooks, reference material which
can be consulted only in the library, and reserved books for use in
the library and for overnight circulation. It is not recommended
that materials from the classroom collections be loaned to pupils
for home use. Such procedure makes for complications in circulation routines and adds to the teacher's burden. Materials needed
by pupils for study at home should be left in the library for whatever type of circulation seems desirable to the teacher and librarian. However, where circulation from classroom collections is
allowed, the books may be supplied with colored cards for such
circulation, while the white card charged to the teacher remains
in the library.

The librarian should work closely with teachers in arranging
for classroom collections at the time needed. If, for instance, the
third grade plans to study Eskimos in February or the tenth grade
in American history will get to the "Period of Big Business" in
April, the librarian should know well in advance in order to
assure that materials will be available. Often materials in great
demand and subject to call from several teachers may have to be
assigned on a definite schedule. It sometimes happens that a
teacher will need to change the time when his class wishes to study
a topic; indeed, he may have to change the topic, if materials
are not available.

Classroom collections should be made available by all school
libraries. Such service is also provided by many public libraries,
either through childrens' rooms or special school collections.
Many school systems, city and county, have centralized collections
of materials which are made available on a system-wide basis to
schools through the library or to individual classrooms. Classroom
collections largely supplant classroom libraries, popular years ago
in many schools, especially on the elementary level, and are in
many ways preferable to them. There are many classrooms which
have additional material, largely of a reference nature, which
belongs to them, even in schools which have centralized libraries.

DAILY RECORD

Date

BOOK CIRCULATION			
General Works - -	000		
Philosophy - - -	100		
Religion - - -	200		
Social Sciences - -	300		
Language - - -	400		
Science - - -	500		
Useful Arts - -	600		
Fine Arts - - -	700		
Literature - - -	800		
History - -	900-909 930-999		
Travel - - -	910-919		
Biography - -	B-920		
Periodicals - - -			
Pamphlets - - -			
Total Non-Fiction - -			
Fiction - - - -			
Rental Collection - -			
Foreign Books - -			
Total Book Circulation			

Signature

(Over)

FIGURE 28a
Printed circulation slip

FIGURE 28b
Printed circulation slip (reverse)

CIRCULATION— OTHER MATERIAL		
Pictures - - -		
Clippings - - -		
Films - - - -		
Records - - -		
Sheet Music - - -		
Total - - - -		

OTHER DAILY STATISTICS		

GAYLORD NO. 1 — PRINTED IN U.S.A.

Count and Filing

At various places in the discussion of routines for circulating various types of materials, it has been suggested that cards for all materials circulated each day be counted, recorded, and filed in such a way that the cards may be easily consulted on demand.

Recording Circulation

A supply of slips for recording daily circulation should be on hand at the desk. Such slips may be purchased from a library supply house, printed locally, or mimeographed in the school office. The form of the daily circulation slip will depend on the information needed for the permanent circulation record kept in a loose-leaf notebook.

While school libraries do not emphasize circulation statistics as do other libraries, especially public libraries, some record of circulation is helpful in indicating types of materials in demand. The daily circulation slip may consist of a simple recording of fiction books, non-fiction books, and non-book materials or a detailed record of non-fiction books by the various classes of the Dewey Decimal Classification and non-book materials separated into audio-visual materials, magazines, pictures, and vertical-file materials. The circulation slip shown in (Figures 28a and 28b) is obtainable from most dealers in library supplies, and is also used by many school libraries. A slip may also be prepared to suit the needs of the school library, such as the slip shown in Figure 29.

Count of circulation should be made at the end of each day or early next morning, certainly before circulation of materials begins again, and the cards filed in proper sequence. Cards for the day's circulation will have been kept together, either in front of the circulation tray or behind the guide card bearing date due of regular 2-week books circulated that day.

Cards should first be separated according to date due. This is where it helps to have different colors of cards for various types of materials. For instance, cards for regular 2-week books will be placed with p-slips for pictures, since they bear a date two weeks from the current date. Cards for renewals, designated by a paper

```
┌─────────────────────────────────────────────┐
│                Daily Record                   │
│  Date _____          │
│  Class:                  No. circ.            │
│  Philosophy (100)        _____          │
│  Religion (200)                               │
│  Social sciences (300)                        │
│  Languages (400)                              │
│  Pure Science (500)                           │
│  Useful arts (600)                            │
│  Arts & recreation (700)                      │
│  Literature (800)                             │
│  History & travel (900)                       │
│  Biography (B & 920)                          │
│     Total non-fiction                         │
│     Total fiction                             │
│  Magazines                                    │
│  Pictures                                     │
│  Vertical File                                │
│  Audio-Visuals                                │
└─────────────────────────────────────────────┘
```

FIGURE 29
Circulation slip suitable for school library

clip, and for magazines will be kept together because they bear a date one week hence. Vertical file material and short-time loans, due three days from the current date, will constitute another group. Blue cards for reserves and all materials charged to teachers will bear the current date, further distinguished because the date will be stamped in a different color.

Count is then made according to the type of materials circulated and entered in pencil on the daily circulation slip. Care should be exercised to keep separate the cards for various lengths of loan. However, if it seems simpler, the count may be made before the cards and slips are separated according to date due. Each librarian will work out the routine for counting which seems most suitable for his library.

As time permits, and as part of an assistant's duty, record should be made on the permanent circulation record (Figure 30). Some librarians prefer to reserve the making of the record for themselves since it gives opportunity for a quick survey of circulation facts and figures. The daily circulation record slips may well be kept for a week or so, just in case it is necessary to consult them, before they are discarded.

Filing Cards

Cards for reserved books which are to be returned early in the morning following date of circulation should not be filed in the circulation file but kept at the front of the circulation tray for quick and easy handling when books are returned.

Nor do cards for all materials charged to teachers, according to the scheme suggested earlier, go into the regular circulation file. Instead, these cards are filed under the name of each teacher taking out materials. For easy handling of cards, however, they should be filed behind the guide cards bearing teachers' names in the same order as cards are filed under date due in the regular circulation file. Since audio-visual materials will normally be charged only to teachers, cards for them will be filed under teachers' names.

Under each date due in the circulation file and in the teachers' file, cards are always filed in the same order. Coming first will be cards for one type of book, either fiction or non-fiction depending on which type constitutes the heavier circulation in a particular school. Cards for the other type will then come together, separated from the first group of cards by colored cards for magazines and vertical file materials. Slips for pictures should come last in

Record of Circulation

Name of School Library ___A.B.C. School for Boys___

Month __March, 1958__

Date	100	200	300	400	500	600	700	800	900	B & 920	Mag.	Pic.	V.F.	A.V.	Total N.F.	Fic-tion
3																
4																
5																
6																
7																
10																
11																
12																
13																
14																
17																
18																
19																
20																
21																
24																
25																
26																
27																
28																
31																
Total																

Remarks

FIGURE 30

Permanent record of circulation

each daily file because they can stand less handling than the cards. With such an arrangement, the assistant can go directly to the appropriate group of cards.

As to the order for filing, slips for pictures are arranged alphabetically by the name of the borrower printed at the top. Magazine cards are arranged alphabetically by the title of the magazine. Cards for vertical file material and for audio-visual materials are simply kept together as a group since there seems to be no suitable way in which to file them. For these cards, it will always be necessary to identify the charge when looking for the card corresponding to the returned material.

Cards for regular books may be arranged in any one of three ways: by call number, alphabetically either by author or title, or by accession number. Filing by call number has the advantage of teaching assistants to work with call numbers and presents an arrangement of cards more nearly related to that of the books on the shelves. An alphabetical arrangement proves easier to handle for many pupils already accustomed to using dictionaries, indexes, and perhaps the card catalog. Many librarians in elementary schools file cards in the circulation file alphabetically by title since pupils usually know and call for books by title. However, if the trend to begin many book titles with the same words ("All about," "First Book," "Real Book," You and") continues, pupil assistants in the elementary schools will find it increasingly difficult to file by title. Others favor arrangement of cards by the accession number because it is simple and easily handled by all pupils. Also, since the accession number must always be verified before any card is returned to the book pocket, the assistant finds the card and checks the accession number in the same operation. Each school librarian should feel free to adopt whatever system of filing insures the quick and accurate finding of the card and returning it to the book.

Attention is called to the seemingly obvious fact that all cards for materials circulated on the same day are not filed under the same date due but under dates indicated on each book card. For instance, cards for materials circulated on October 1 would be distributed as follows: Regular or 2-week books and slips for pictures under October 15; short-time loans or 3-day books and vertical file material, October 4; magazines and renewals for one week only, October 8. Under the stated date due, each file would always be set up in the same order, according to the plan adopted by the library, as discussed in the preceding paragraph. In libraries where certain types of materials are not circulated, cards for them would not be present in the file, of course, and filing would accordingly be simplified.

Circulation Simplified for Elementary School Libraries

The detailed discussion of filing cards and other routines applies largely to the circulation of materials in the high school library. Both policy and procedures may be greatly simplified for the elementary school library.

There will be little or no use for books to be placed on reserve in the library. Materials for a special unit or project will be available through classroom collections borrowed from the library by the teacher. Only one period of loan, one week if pupils are scheduled to the library once a week, will be necessary. When classes are scheduled more frequently, it is advised that books be charged out on only one designated day. Since elementary books are usually slight and quickly read, there should be little demand for renewals. The scheduled day would serve as a constant reminder that books are due, so that there should be few overdues and consequently small fines. In fact, many elementary school libraries have no system of fines. Personal reserves may be dispensed with since elementary pupils are not usually pushed for assignments. Pictures would probably constitute the only type of non-book material loaned to pupils.

Instead of maintaining an elaborate circulation file, a simple method of recording circulation is to hold together with a rubber band all book cards charged to a class. Each pupil will have written his name and homeroom number on the card on which the date due is stamped. To further identify the loan, a symbol (4 S designating Miss Smith's fourth grade) should be lettered beside the date due on each date-due slip. Then, whether the book is returned singly or with the group, its card may be easily located in the file. Within each group, cards may be filed alphabetically by author or title, or by accession number according to the library policy. (Filing by call number is not suggested for elementary school libraries since it is more difficult for pupil assistants.) The group of cards is then placed behind the guide card indicating the date due. Count should be made before the cards are filed each day and transferred to a permanent record.

Whenever an elementary school library needs more elaborate routines and records, the ones suggested elsewhere in this chapter may be easily adapted for use.

Overdue Books and Other Materials

No matter how much effort is made by the library staff to get materials returned on time, there will still be a certain number of readers who keep books overtime. Overdue books will be found charged to a relatively few pupils using the library and most likely to the same ones repeatedly.

In a school library where books are constantly in demand, it is recommended that a book should be handled as overdue if not returned the day it is due. This is in contrast to other libraries that wait for a specified time before sending out overdue notices. Each morning, after all returned books have been checked in, a pupil assistant removes from the file dated the previous day all cards for books which have not been returned. It is well first to take the cards to the shelves to make sure the corresponding books have not been shelved without cards. The name and homeroom of each pupil having an overdue book is then obtained from the book cards. Notices are made out (Figure 31) and sent to the pupil in study hall or, through the homeroom representative, to his homeroom. It is not advisable unless absolutely necessary to burden teachers with distribution of library notices since they have such a multiplicity of duties already.

After the notices have been prepared, a check in pencil is placed on each card beside the date due to indicate that the first notice has been sent. Cards may then be returned to the circula-

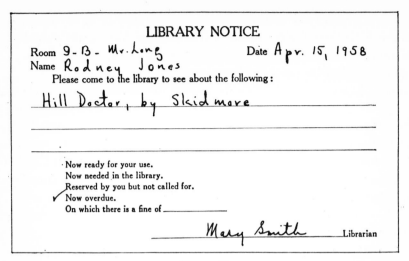

FIGURE 31

Notice for book overdue

tion file or filed together behind a guide marked "Overdues," separated by dates on which the books were due. This latter arrangement necessitates a second group of guide cards by dates but prevents cards for books long overdue from being filed in the live circulation file.

At the end of a week, if some of the books have still not been returned, a second notice, so marked in red, is prepared and sent to the student and a check mark in red is placed beside the date due on the book card to indicate that a second notice has been sent.

When a second week has passed and a book is still overdue, the book card should be given to the librarian who will either write or have the principal write a letter to the parents of the pupil urging that the book be returned and stating the amount of fine already due. The letter should also inform the parents how much the book will cost if it is lost and must be replaced. This amount can be taken from the book card or from the record in the accession book. It is suggested that the fine accrued on a book never exceed the cost of replacing the book.

Many schools have the regulation that pupils may not receive report cards at certain stated periods in the school year if all obligations have not been met. This would include return of all overdue books, or payment for them if lost, and fines owed to the library. In such schools, overdues will need to be handled again, and statements prepared, at the time for distributing report cards and at the end of the semester. Certainly every effort should be made to retrieve overdue books, or secure payment for them, and collect all fines before the end of each school year. While the above-mentioned regulation might not stand legal testing, it is a great help to the school librarian. The library should be notified when pupils drop out of school so that a check may be made on materials charged to them.

Whenever a lost book is paid for, notation "Lost and paid" or "L & pd." should be placed on the shelf-list card beside the accession number for the lost book. Consideration is then given as to whether the book is to be replaced or withdrawn from the collection, as discussed in Chapter 5.

Fines in the School Library

Library literature is replete with articles for and against the use of fines in the school library. The purpose of fines, of course, is to get materials returned to the library as promptly as possible and, if a school library can accomplish this feat without the use of fines, and the special records they require, so much the better. Overdue books are not such a problem with elementary school pupils, who come regularly to the library by classes, and many elementary school libraries do not charge fines. Some high school libraries also do not charge fines.

The substitute for fines most often suggested is to have the offending pupils work in the library to make up for keeping books overtime. The plan tends to work out better in theory than practice. Usually the pupil who habitually keeps books until they are overdue is apt to be careless in other phases of his school work. A busy school librarian has no time to teach such pupils how to perform library duties, or to supervise their working in the library.

Since fines are customary in most libraries, there seems no valid reason why they should not be used in school libraries as well. Most pupils are able to pay small fines; if not, some arrangement can be made to take care of fines when pupils are not able to pay them. It is suggested that fines be kept to a minimum charge and always, except in hardship cases, be collected. The following would seem reasonable charges for overdue materials in a school library:

> Regular books (2 weeks)—1 cent per day, 5 cents per week
> Short-time loans (3 days)—5 cents per day, 25 cents per week
> Reserved books (overnight)—10 cents per day
> Magazines (7 days)—2 cents per day, 10 cents per week for each issue
> Vertical file material (3 days)—5 cents per package per day
> Pictures (2 weeks)—5 cents per package per day

It is much better if fines are paid when the materials are returned to the library, and every effort should be made to catch overdues at the desk and to collect fines immediately. But many pupils contrive to return overdue materials when no assistant is watching, or send them by someone else to avoid facing the issue. This is one disadvantage, of course, in having books returned to the library by homeroom representatives, rather than by individual pupils. Homeroom representatives should be instructed to check for overdue books before leaving the homeroom and make the pupil who borrowed the book responsible for going to the library to pay the fine. It is not advisable to have homeroom representative collect fines and pay them in the library.

Record of Fines

If a reader's card is used in the library, a record of the fine on each transaction will be noted on the pupil's card (Figure 32). This is an argument for using the reader's card. Some school libraries which do not keep readers' cards for all pupils maintain a similar file for students who seem prone to keep books overtime and thus run up fines.

LIBRARY		
A BC School for Boys		
BORROWER'S NAME		
Brown, Tom		
ROOM		
Miss Manley — 10 - A		
DATE DUE	TITLE	DATE RETURNED
Mar, 31	*Storm over the land*	*10¢* *Apr. 14*
	GAYLORD 132	

FIGURE 32

Record of fine on reader's card

Whenever a book is returned to the desk overdue and the fine is not paid because the pupil is not present, a fine slip is made out (Figure 33) and sent to him either in study hall or by his homeroom representative. In case either a reader's card or a fine card is used, the record of the fine owed should be made on that card. When a fine is paid, credit is given by marking "pd." beside the amount due. At intervals, the cards should be consulted for fines that are allowed to accumulate. This routine may be simplified by using a colored signal to indicate unpaid fines. Some libraries require pupils to pay fines accumulated to a certain amount, 50 cents or more, before allowing them to borrow further materials. This is a difficult regulation to enforce in a library where materials are needed for school assignments. Sometimes, as in the case of books long overdue, it is necessary to write a letter to parents regarding unpaid fines.

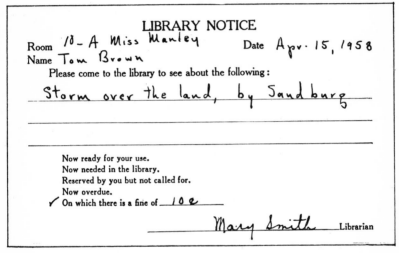

FIGURE 33

Fine slip made out to be sent to reader

If neither a reader's card nor a fine card is kept, the simplest method of recording unpaid fines is to use a special notebook, pages of which are prepared to record the following information: Name of pupil, homeroom, brief title of book, date due, date returned, and fine owed. It is well also for the assistant to pencil in the space for title "Left on desk," "Found in principal's office" or "Returned by homeroom representative," etc., as the case may be (Figure 34). When a pupil comes to pay a fine, or perhaps to contend that he does not owe one, the full record is in the fine notebook and can be located by his name. As the fine is paid, a line can be drawn through the record and when all records on

Name of pupil	Homeroom	Title of book	Date due	Date returned	Fine
Joe Tate	11-A Miss Sisk	Iron Duke	Apr. 1	Apr. 14	10¢
Anne Carroll	10-B Mr. Dean	Returned by home-room representative No time for tears	Apr. 8	Apr. 16	12¢

FIGURE 34

Page from book for recording fines when reader's card is not used the page are completed by payment, the page may be removed. At intervals fine notices will be made out and sent to pupils whose fines have not been paid.

Another simple record helpful in handling fines is a daily slip record of fines collected (Figure 35). This is kept in the fine drawer. The school librarian should put a certain amount of money in suitable change in the fine drawer each morning. If the

```
┌─────────────────────────────────────────────┐
│                                               │
│         Daily record of fines:                │
│                                               │
│                 Date April 1, 1958            │
│                                               │
├─────────────────────────────────────────────┤
│  1st period:   5¢   7¢   10¢   24¢            │
│  16¢   6¢                                      │
│                                               │
├─────────────────────────────────────────────┤
│  2d period:                                   │
│                                               │
│                                               │
│                                               │
├─────────────────────────────────────────────┤
│  3d period:                                   │
│                                               │
│                                               │
│                                               │
├─────────────────────────────────────────────┤
│  4th period:                                  │
│                                               │
│                                               │
│                                               │
├─────────────────────────────────────────────┤
│  6th period:                                  │
│                                               │
│                                               │
│                                               │
└─────────────────────────────────────────────┘
```

FIGURE 35
Daily record of fines collected

amount is $5, the daily record of fines collected, as indicated on the fine slip, plus $5 should be the total amount of money in the drawer at the end of the day. The amount above five dollars will, of course, represent fines taken in for that day and should tally with the amount recorded on the fine slip.

Most schools allow the library to keep any fines collected as a fund for the purchase of items not included in the library budget. Some require that fine money be deposited in a general fund kept in the school office. A school librarian who does spend fine money directly should keep records to show exactly how such funds are spent, as discussed in Chapter 6.

Damages to Library Materials

As has been previously suggested, all materials in circulation should be examined on return for damages beyond normal wear and tear. If this is done regularly by all assistants, the problem of fixing blame for damages will be greatly simplified. Materials with minor damages, such as a few torn pages, loose leaves, or a missing pocket or date-due slip, should be laid aside for mending according to suggestions in Chapter 5. Efforts to collect payment for such minor damages are time-consuming and are apt to make for bad relations with readers.

Major damages should be paid for by the reader to whom the book was last charged. Included in the category of major damages would be a section of pages torn or cut from a book, a generous amount of crayon marks that are almost impossible to remove, or evidence that the material has been in the possession of a puppy or a younger brother or sister in the chewing stage. Usually major damages make the material unsuitable for further use, with the result that replacement cost should be charged. The library should form a policy regarding charges to be made and enter decisions in the circulation manual so that assistants at the desk will have authority for charges. It seems reasonable to charge for books, magazines, and other purchased materials the amount paid for each since that sum will be needed to replace them. In the case of vertical file material and mounted pictures, a nominal sum of 5 to 10 cents might be charged for each item, since both materials and time have gone into their preparation for use. The prices of books and pamphlets may be obtained from the trade entry (source, date and price on the page following the title page) when the book is in hand, from the book card when the material itself is missing, or in any case from the accession book. The price of an issue of a magazine can be obtained usually from the cover. Pupil assistants should consult the librarian regarding damaged materials not covered by the manual, and whenever the amount due is questioned.

Circulation Manual

Reference has been made to a manual of library policies and routines. This manual should be in a loose-leaf binder, and should be added to and altered as additions and changes become necessary. It should always be available at the circulation desk for reference use by pupil assistants. The circulation manual should include such information as hours when the library is open; regulations for the use of library materials (that is, which ones circulate, and for what lengths of loan); policies regarding such problems as overdues, fines, lost and damaged materials; and definite routines for the circulation of various types of materials. In effect, the circulation manual might well be a brief version, in outline form, of this chapter, geared to the policies, routines, and records of the individual school library. A table of contents and an index will greatly facilitate its use. Pupil assistants should be urged to study the manual and refer to it whenever questions as to "how-to-do-it" arise. They should also be instructed to consult the librarian about matters not covered by the circulation manual.

Conclusion

Circulation of materials in any library is an important part of the work. In the school library, most of the circulation duties must be performed by pupil assistants carefully chosen and constantly supervised. For this reason definite policies should be formed and followed and simple routines established. A circulation manual at the desk is a helpful guide which answers most questions for student assistants. The manual covers circulation routines and records which should be as few and simple as possible and free from red tape. Both teachers and pupils should be given ample opportunity to know the essential regulations of the library and the reasons for them. Such regulations are then followed in the same manner regardless of the circumstances under which material is being borrowed. The wheels of circulation should turn constantly and with as little friction as possible if the library is to operate efficiently.

CHAPTER 4

THE USE OF MATERIALS IN THE SCHOOL LIBRARY

Introduction

The preceding chapter discussed in some detail the circulation of library materials and the activities which center around the circulation desk. It was suggested that most of the routines outlined could be performed by pupil assistants, carefully chosen and trained, with close supervision from the librarian. In an effort to give a well-rounded picture of the school library at work, the present chapter deals with the use of materials in the school library and emphasizes the role of the librarian in promoting library use.

School Library Attendance

Pupil use of the school library is determined largely by the level served, the use made of library materials to enrich the curriculum, and the amount of free time which the pupils devote to reading in the library. There are, of course, elementary school, junior high school, and senior high school libraries with various combinations of the three levels. A fairly recent development is the library which serves all twelve grades of a combined school. With the increasing trend toward consolidation of schools, larger enrollments are the pattern and attendance increases accordingly in the library which serves all pupils of the school.

In the elementary school and sometimes in the junior high school, attendance in the library is regularly scheduled. Each class in turn has a definite time once a week or oftener when the group goes to the library, accompanied by the teacher. There the pupils return books borrowed at the last library period, select and charge out other books and engage in some library activity, such as hearing a story told or read. They may have a free reading period for browsing at will among the many appealing

books and magazines. Sometimes, especially if the class is beginning a unit of study, or climaxing work on a unit with all sorts
of activities, pupils will use their library period to do reference
work. Whatever the activity, both teacher and librarian must
work closely together to make the library period meaningful. To
this end, the teacher should remain with his pupils and not treat
the library period as a free period.

Often, during a regular class period, a small group of pupils
in elementary grades may be given permission to work on a
special topic in the school library. Or, when several pupils have
already performed the tasks at hand, they may be allowed time
in the library for additional free reading, a highly desirable practice especially for the superior readers. In assuring that there
will be space in the library for such unscheduled pupils, the
teacher must work closely with the librarian who has similar
requests from other groups.

In high schools, where attendance in the library is usually
not scheduled, pupils go to the library largely during their study
hall periods. In some high schools and unfortunately in some not
so small, the library is also used as a study hall, to which some
or all of the pupils who are free from classes at any given period
are scheduled. This is by no means desirable because it usually
results in crowding. Furthermore, pupils are then in the library
from compulsion rather than choice, a fact which often leads to
problems in discipline. The librarian must consequently devote
more than a proportionate amount of his time and attention to
the relatively few problem pupils, so that there is no opportunity
to help the many pupils who are there for actual use of library
materials. As a result, the situation is more like that of a study
hall than a school library.

The presence of a teacher, generally required by school library standards when the number of pupils assigned to the library
runs above a designated figure, does not always solve discipline
problems. On the contrary, additional problems may arise from
the dual control of teacher and librarian.

The most common situation, however, is for the high school
library to be separate from but adjoining the study hall with free

passage to and from the library as pupils need to use library materials. In theory, this seems an excellent arrangement and one fairly easy to administer. There are differences of opinion as to what constitutes legitimate library attendance. If the concept of the library as a place where pupils go to *make use of library materials* is held throughout the school, many problems concerned with library attendance will be solved.

Pupils should not be allowed to go to the library merely to be together, whether to study or just talk. Some use it to kill time, spending the entire period reading comic strips in the daily paper, leafing through a current magazine, or just sitting before an open book. Others use the library purely for study, possibly because the library atmosphere is more conducive to real study than that of the study hall. Nevertheless, if the library is conceived of as the place *reserved for the use of library materials,* then pupils who only want to solve a problem in mathematics, translate Latin, or study punctuation rules may reasonably be required to remain in study hall. The important factor in library attendance is that pupils who need to use library materials may have easy access to them and that the librarian be free to assist the pupils in locating materials.

It is a good plan to limit the use of the library to only one visit during a given period for any pupil. He should understand that it is his privilege to spend a few minutes or the entire period in the library, depending on the extent of his need for library materials, but that once he has returned to the study hall, he should remain there. This regulation is also helpful in teaching the pupil to plan his visit to the school library so as to reap the maximum benefit.

It seems reasonable also to expect pupils to read material that is in the library collection while they are in the school library. Such a regulation will prevent the tendency of some pupils to bring to the library in large notebooks favorite comic books, sensational paper backs, or other material unrelated to selected school library materials. In occupying space in the library for such reading, they may prevent some other pupils who need to use library materials from doing so.

In addition to individual pupil attendance from the study hall, a teacher often wishes to bring an entire high school class to work in the library on a project. Group attendance should always be arranged well in advance with the librarian so that space may be provided and needed materials assembled. Otherwise, time will be wasted and confusion caused while the librarian, teacher and pupils "mill around" to locate materials. The teacher should always remain with the class to direct the project on which the group is working, to select the material best suited to the needs of the various pupils, and to control the behavior of his group in the library. The librarian is thus freed to work with other pupils using library materials.

If conference space is not available, a group of adjoining tables in the reading room should be provided so that pupils and the teacher may work together without unduly disturbing other library users. It may well be that when an entire class is working in the library, individual attendance from the study hall should be limited to those who need to use library materials for the next day's classes.

Occasionally high school pupils will wish to come from a classroom in a small group either because they need to work together on a project or because they have completed whatever the class is doing. Prior arrangement should be made with the librarian even for such a small group. When the group wishes to work together, available conference space is preferable to the reading room. Such a working group appreciates being able to leave materials on assigned shelves in a conference room for continued use if the project extends over several days.

Checking Library Attendance

Even when the actual taking of attendance is not the librarian's responsibility, it is well to keep at least an occasional sampling of attendance. This could be done for one period each day, the first period on Monday, second on Tuesday, etc., or for all periods during one day, changing the day in successive weeks. This checking may be done quietly by a pupil assistant seated near the door to count all who enter. Even the librarian will probably be surprised at the number served in a given period. Such information is always good for library reports, discussed in a later chapter, and may strengthen requests for additional space or more professional help.

From time to time, it is desirable to have each pupil sign his name on a sheet of paper posted beside the exit and note how long he was in the library and what specific use he made of library materials. This not only gives the librarian and teachers an idea of what use is made of the library but may cause pupils themselves to consider whether or not they are using the library to advantage. This device should not be used so often that it becomes a tiresome exercise, and pupils should understand the purpose of the resulting record. If teachers could sometimes encourage pupils to write compositions on what use they make of library materials, the same purpose would be served.

Activities of the School Library

It is difficult to visualize what actually goes on in a busy school library because the picture changes so rapidly and presents so many different facets. No period of the day is the same as any other, nor does one day duplicate yesterday's activities or necessarily reflect what tomorrow's program may be. It is this quality which makes school library work both interesting and challenging but, at the same time, difficult. No one promises an easy life to school librarians and any librarians who find school library work less than demanding are certain to be denying pupils and teachers their inalienable right to good library service. There are so many satisfactions in school library work that those who have chosen it prefer it to all other kinds of library work.

In any given period of a school day, many of the following activities are likely to be in progress in the library: borrowing and returning of materials at the circulation desk; browsing at the shelves or among books ready to be shelved for new selections; reading of newspapers, magazines, and books; obtaining materials from the reserved book shelves for class assignments;

consultation of the card catalog; use of reference books, especially dictionaries and encyclopedias; checking of periodical indexes followed by requests for magazines needed to find cited articles; perusal of maps and atlases; and appeals to the librarian for help in locating materials for a difficult assignment. Pupil assistants will not only be working at the desk, as suggested in Chapter 3, but will also be reading shelves and arranging books on them in the reading room. In the work room others will be mending books, typing book lists, preparing books and other materials for use, or getting materials ready for storage. Group work will be in progress at a reading room table, in a conference room or both. In the elementary school library, a group is hearing a story told or read. Someone may be examining material from the vertical file or picture collection as to suitability for use. A teacher may have sent for a desired filmstrip and its accompanying projector.

The librarian is probably hoping for a moment to check the bibliographical data for a few stray items needed to complete the next book order now in preparation. He will be lucky if, in addition to repeated requests from pupils, he does not have to answer a request from a classroom, either for information or materials, or decide with a teacher when a group may come for work in the library. Perhaps a teacher has returned a classroom collection and wishes to select books for the new unit which his class is beginning. "Never a dull moment" could easily describe school library activities and the librarian's efforts to direct them.

Reading Guidance

By and large, however, the school librarian spends most of the school day doing reading guidance and reference work. Indeed, these two activities are the librarian's highest contribution to the school program.

Reading guidance in the school library is the sum total of all activities by which the librarian attempts to encourage all pupils to read freely and widely that they may experience the satisfaction which comes alone from reading good books. The activity may be as simple as helping a reader to find "another good book," or arranging a simple bulletin board display of new book jackets. It may be the combination of an elaborate exhibit of books with a program for Book Week. Reading guidance includes many group activities: showing a picture book, telling a story, reading poetry aloud, giving a book talk, taking a group of new books to a classroom for presentation. Reading guidance also involves working closely with individual readers, particularly those with reading problems.

Indeed, much of what the librarian does is aimed at stimulating in pupils the desire to read and to find books that are right for them. Reading guidance in the final essence is simply bringing the reader and book together—a gratifying experience as any librarian knows. To achieve this union, books in the collection should be well selected and organized for efficient use, as emphasized in earlier chapters. The librarian should know both books and readers and be adept in suiting books to readers. He should also be given the time he needs for this important task.

There is a feeling in some quarters that the school library should concentrate on reference work and reading connected with the curriculum, leaving guidance in leisure reading as the function of the public library. This theory breaks down in the areas where there is little or no public library service. Many pupils never see books except on the shelves of the school library. Unfortunately, many schools, especially on the elementary level, have no libraries and their pupils no access to library materials. But even if public library service were everywhere available, the school library would still have to provide guidance for the large percentage of pupils in any community who never go to the public library. Besides, the needs of the reader in a school library may be satisfied immediately; he is not obliged to wait until he can make a trip to the public library, or, in rural areas, until the bookmobile is scheduled to make its next appearance.

Reading guidance is, then, extremely important in a school library and presents an almost unparalleled opportunity. No other librarian has all the children of school age from a community as potential library users, usually under the same roof as the library itself, day after day, year after year. There are school records to help the librarian understand pupils and their problems. The school librarian has the benefit of teachers with whom to discuss pupils, a helpful experience for both since they work with the same pupils in slightly different relationships. He also has fairly easy contact with parents of the pupils through parent-teacher organizations and other group meetings which bring parents to school. It may well be that through the school library pupils learn to depend on or to reject library service. To the end that they may become library users, the librarian attempts to help the reader not only to understand how to use the library but also to evaluate materials so that he may select good reading for himself.

Contrary to belief in some quarters, books and other materials, in the school library as in other libraries, must be taken to the readers. Though many pupils do visit the library regularly and use its materials judiciously, many others never enter the library unless scheduled there or forced to go by a classroom assignment. The indifferent reader must be met with an atmosphere of help-fulness in the effort to get him to read. The inexpert reader must be helped to find something in his field of interest and encouraged to read something better. The good reader must be supplied with materials to satisfy his present needs and, at the same time, to make him climb a little higher on the reading ladder. A great deal more attention should be given to the needs of the superior reader, as will be pointed out later in the chapter.

Wide Variety of Materials

For an adequate program of reading guidance, the school library must have a wide variety of reading materials for all reading interests, at all reading levels, and for all stages of maturity. Normal children not only possess the group interests common to their own age and grade but reveal rather early other reading interests peculiarly their own. Materials are needed on a wide variety of subjects both for curriculum needs and for in-dividual reading interests. Indeed it is almost impossible to sepa-rate the reading that a pupil does for a curriculum need from that which he does on his own. A book of historical fiction which fits into the period of history being currently studied may prove to be the most thrilling reading the pupil ever does. He chooses the biography of a scientist because of his own interest and finds that it enriches a report which he is preparing for a science class. A book read purely for pleasure helps the pupil in his over-all adjustment to living and working with the members of his school group.

In any school grade, there are sure to be at least three levels of reading ability: pupils who are reading at the correct grade level, those who are reading below and those who are reading above. It is possible, for instance, in a sixth grade to have not only sixth-grade readers who will normally constitute the majority, but some who can read only third-grade materials and a few superior readers who read materials aimed at ninth-grade reading level. Educators say that it is possible to have as many as eight levels of reading ability in a group of upper elementary pupils. Thus the school library must provide material on all reading levels if the pupils are to read with satisfaction.

Maturity also plays a great part in children's reading. Two girls, both aged eleven, in the same grade and with identical I.Q.'s may because of differences in social maturity be miles apart in their reading. One might conceivably still be playing with dolls and clinging to the reading of fairy stories and modern fantasies, while the other is attending prom parties and asking eagerly at the circulation desk for "teen-age" books, hoping for even a slight romance. The school librarian must recognize individual differences in readers and provide for them in the library collection.

Types of Readers

The school library because it has all the pupils gets all types of readers. Many in the school are non-readers. It may be well to comment here on the fact that teachers and librarians have a somewhat different interpretation of the term "non-reader." By "non-reader" the educator means simply one who cannot read. The librarian means that he does not read. The reader who cannot read has not mastered the mechanics of reading. The reader who can read but does not has not formed the habit of reading. And reading is a habit in which no one indulges unless the act of reading repays him in genuine satisfaction. It is the constant concern of the teacher that all pupils learn to read. The librarian hopes to develop the habit of reading by finding for pupils as they learn to read something worth-while and interesting on which to practice their newly acquired skill.

Overlapping with "non-readers," in whatever sense the word is used, are poor or slow readers. Because they find little or no enjoyment in reading, they avoid it and substitute other activities for reading, even in the learning process. Poor readers need special help in their reading difficulties, so that the librarian must work closely with parents and teachers. The chief service which the librarian can render is to make available material that is simply written on subjects of interest to poor readers who are often older than their classmates.

Many other readers are indolent—just plain lazy. They visit the library only when forced to by a class assignment. They consult a reference book or book on reserve and are careful to do no reading beyond the assigned pages. When a book report is due, the indolent reader searches diligently for a "thin book" to meet the requirement. Such readers may also be slow readers or on the way to being poor readers because they practice reading so little— seldom if ever for pure enjoyment. The librarian tries to find a thin book that is interesting and full of adventure in hopes it may encourage the pupil to read other books as well.

One group may be classified as "lop-sided" readers because they read too many books of only one kind. Thus they miss out on the broadening influence of books in many fields. What a lop-sided reader does read may be quite worth-while but it is always fiction, often confined to one type of fiction, or always biography or science. A reader of this class may decide on a career in line with his interest. He should be helped to realize that he will be a better doctor or just a better person for having read widely in other fields.

There are a few pupils who might be termed inveterate readers: those who may read to excess and in so doing neglect their
school work or avoid contacts with other people. Sometimes the
librarian spots such readers from repeated handling of book cards
bearing signatures or from constant replacement of the reader's
cards as each fills up from use. More often they are called to the
librarian's attention by a teacher who complains that such readers
are not doing scholastic work of which they are capable, or by
parents who are not pleased with the current school report and
are prone to blame the library since their children seem always
to be reading. On rare occasions, the principal may request that
such pupils be limited in their use of the school library until
there is improvement in scholastic standing.

The large majority of pupils, however, are good readers.
They read on their normal reading level, are interested in various
subjects, and read a wide variety of types of books. In fact, it is
difficult to find a good book they do not like. They return one
book and express satisfaction as they browse to find another.
Sometimes they decide not to take a book because of pressure of
study but are back again as soon as the push is over. Good readers are the joy of every librarian's heart. One must be careful
neither to spend too much time with them nor, on the other hand,
neglect them for the problem readers, on the assumption that
good readers need no help.

There are also, as suggested earlier, some superior readers
who are capable of reading far beyond their age or grade level.
Often their need is for more mature reading material. In the
lower grades, this need may be met by selecting books for
superior readers from books intended for older pupils. In the
senior high school library, however, there is a challenge for
teachers and the librarian to include well-chosen adult books in
the collection. Fortunately there is more help than formerly for
choosing adult materials suitable for high school readers. "The
Outlook Tower," a regular section in *The Horn Book* contributed
by Margaret Scoggin, Coordinator of Young Adult Services in the
New York Public Library, suggests suitable adult books for young
people and a few teen-age books. *The Booklist and Subscription*

Books Bulletin performs a similar service by indicating which of the new books reviewed in the adult section are suitable for use with young people. A recent list for this purpose is *Book Bait* (American Library Association, 1957) with the sub-title "detailed notes on adult books popular with young people," compiled by Elinor Walker of the Carnegie Library, Pittsburgh, for the Association of Young People's Librarians.

The group of superior readers may easily be neglected, especially if they fail to make their demands vocal. When this happens, they may attempt to satisfy their desire for more mature materials by turning to the lighter type of books which because of adult demand must be made available at the public library or to more sensational books from the rental collection of the corner drug store. An excellent opportunity presents itself for teachers of senior high school pupils to suggest adult books which they would like their pupils to read and to solicit cooperation from both the school librarian and the young people's librarian at the public library in making these books available.

Problems in Reading Guidance

Several problems face the school librarian who attempts to help in reading guidance with all pupils of varied abilities and interests. The first is the problem of time. Many other tasks that must be done regularly clamor for the librarian's time and attention. Reference work, because of the pressure of an assignment for the following day, must take precedence over reading guidance, especially when the desired book is wanted solely to satisfy a personal interest. The result would be frustrating except for the realization that one librarian can accomplish only so much and that some reading guidance is better than none.

The second problem stems from the fact that the librarian is expected to work with all pupils, those who come to the library of their own volition, those who are scheduled there, and those who seldom or never come. The librarian must offer reading guidance to those who are not interested in reading as well as to those who are. The wide variety of materials needed for reading guidance is often not possible in the school library with a limited budget, in the expenditure of which curriculum needs receive primary consideration.

Reading ability, or lack of it, poses another problem for the school librarian who attempts to find material simple enough for pupils to read, yet on their interest level. He must indeed select material for a few pupils who read so poorly that most of the library's material is beyond their ability to read mechanically, much less interpret intelligently. Sometimes reading guidance is the dead serious business of finding *a* book. A sixth-grade boy interested in the Vikings wants something less elementary than a third-grade picture book which is all he can read. A high school boy with a high I.Q. needs really scientific material on aerodynamics, though he may be reading on only junior high level. An eighth-grade girl who would like to enjoy books that others of her class enjoy must be directed to Gertrude Warner's *Boxcar Children* (Scott, Foresman, 1942) because the vocabulary limited to some six hundred words is as much as she can handle. Indeed the school librarian must develop a large measure of ingenuity in fitting together books and readers.

Fortunately material suitable for problem readers becomes increasingly available and there is some guidance in selection for them. A very practical aid is the *High Interest Low Vocabulary Booklist* compiled by Donald D. Durrell and published by the Boston University School of Education (c1952). A few other aids are suggested in the Appendix. An alert school librarian gradually compiles a list of materials suitable for slow readers in the collection of his own school library.

To make time for reading guidance, as well as reference work, the school librarian must turn over to pupil assistants as many routine duties as are consistent with good library service. Many duties which still must be performed by the librarian may sometimes have to be done before or after school or often on Saturday mornings. In spite of the fairly common notion that school libraries have no homework, every librarian knows that books would seldom get ordered except for the checking of booklists done at home. In fact, many books would never get on the shelves if they were not taken home overnight to be cataloged. This does not take into account the endless reading of books for children and young people which any librarian must do in order to advise pupils about their reading. Reading guidance is time consuming but the school librarian must find time for this important phase of his work.

Program of Reading Guidance

It is difficult to outline a routine for reading guidance, which needs to be done largely on an individual basis and yet is so interwoven with all library work. Florence D. Cleary in *Blueprints for Better Reading* (H. W. Wilson Company, 1957) offers some helpful suggestions in Chapter 4, "Organizing Reading Guidance Programs," and devotes Part II of the book to "Programs in Reading Guidance" from which the school librarian can derive direction.

There are certain things which the librarian can do to improve the total program of reading guidance in the school library. Though some of these have already been suggested, they are offered again for emphasis:

1. Build up a well-rounded collection of materials in various fields for all reading abilities, reading interests and levels of maturity. Materials should be selected to meet the needs of the curriculum and be in line with the interests of the pupils of the individual school. They should be chosen with the cooperation of pupils, teachers and administrators.

2. Keep the collection up to date by constant weeding to remove dead wood, by making replacements where needed and by adding new materials to fill gaps and keep the collection balanced.

3. Read books from the collection, study reviews of new books, and discuss titles with other librarians and teachers in an effort to know what books contain and for what specific purpose they may be used. Unless the librarian knows books as well as readers, his efforts to bring the two together will be futile.

4. Study available records in the school which will throw light on individual pupils and their needs.

5. Discuss individual pupils with teachers and parents when reading problems are discovered.

6. Keep a reading file for all pupils, when time permits, certainly for those who present reading problems.

7. Observe children reading in the library to discover any undesirable reading habits or attitudes toward reading and do what can be done to help them.

8. Use bulletin boards, or other means of publicity in the school, to publicize materials that will interest the pupils.

9. Compile brief lists of suggested books for individual readers or groups of readers, keeping copies for use with other pupils who may have similar problems.

10. Provide opportunities in the library for pupils to share book experiences by telling stories or reading aloud to younger children and by discussing books which they have read with other pupils or writing their opinions of books.

11. Introduce books to class groups in an effort to reach pupils who do not come to the library on other occasions.

12. Encourage pupils to request books for purchase and honor such requests as often as is consistent with wise choice and the library budget.

13. As much as time permits, work with individual pupils to meet their own needs and give them the assurance that the librarian is interested in their reading.

Pupils and Reading Guidance

Pupil assistants should be encouraged to read books in the collection and discuss them with the librarian and in meetings of the library club. New books may be made available to pupil assistants, as well as to teachers, before they are offered for general circulation. This is a privilege which pupil assistants appreciate and which gives them a feeling of being members of the library staff. Any pupil assistant can give his own reaction to a book which he has read and suggest its possible appeal to other pupils. A more discerning assistant can offer suggestions as to a book's possible usefulness in the collection. With such aid, the librarian will extend, without actually reading them, his acquaintance with many books as they are added. Pupil assistants can also aid greatly in suggesting at the desk books which will be enjoyed by their fellow pupils.

Indeed, every school librarian recognizes the amount of reading guidance done by the pupils among themselves. Someone wanting a book to read goes to the shelves, takes down book after book, and consults the book card. The name of a chum is often sufficient recommendation for the book to be chosen. On the other hand, a small boy, scanning a list of girls' names on the book card, returns it to the book pocket and the book to the shelf as if afraid to be caught with it. Any librarian recognizes simple reading guidance when he overhears a pupil suggest a book which he has enjoyed to a friend or ask the friend if he has read a certain title and how he enjoyed it before he makes his own choice. This is wholesome, augments the program of reading guidance, and saves recommendation by the librarian when just "another good book to read" is the order.

To capitalize on reading guidance from fellow pupils, it is advisable to keep a file, probably at the desk used by the librarian, of cards prepared by pupils giving their opinion of books read. The larger 4" by 6" cards are better for the purpose than 3" by 5" cards, since pupils will be writing in long hand. At the top of the card, the title of the book, followed by the author's name, should be lettered for easy filing. The pupil writes a brief statement as to the book's contents and his opinion of the book, then signs his name and grade. Pupils enjoy checking this file of titles for suggestions as to what to read next, thus saving both time and energy for the librarian. The file should be weeded periodically because the reviews are more effective if written by pupils who are still in school. The current date should be stamped near the pupil's signature as a guide in withdrawing cards.

The attention of pupils should be directed to the annotation on all Wilson printed cards, particularly helpful when a reader wants to know what a book of fiction "is about" and the title does not so indicate. In the days before Wilson cards, one school librarian typed an annotation giving briefly "who, when, where, what and why" on the author card of every book of fiction cataloged for the collection and found it most helpful. This is suggested for books of fiction for which Wilson cards are not available.

Use should also be made of printed lists, such as those published by the National Council of Teachers of English, which are designed for use by the pupils themselves. (See list of book selection aids in the Appendix.) As time permits, the librarian should compile lists of books on various subjects available in the collection. If these lists are supplied with the call number of each title, put into colorful covers and kept at the circulation desk, pupils will take them to the shelves and choose titles for themselves. Independent choice is helpful in the reading program.

Teachers appreciate the availability in the school library of similar lists of books and parts of books which are in the collection on various topics studied in the classroom. One librarian analyzes all material on American history as it is cataloged and lists it under the period of history to which it belongs. By addition of new materials, deletion of materials no longer available, and revision every several years, a valuable index has evolved. A list which receives constant wear may be protected by placing the pages in plastic folders that are bound in a sturdy notebook.

Reference Work in the School Library

Good reference work is possible only where there is an adequate collection of reference materials with which to work. The backbone of a good reference collection is encyclopedias, chosen for their accuracy, authoritativeness and up-to-dateness. Encyclopedias in every school library should, of course, be on the reading level of the pupils to be served, adult encyclopedias for senior high school libraries only and children's encyclopedias in elementary school libraries. Junior high school libraries, between the other two levels, must often include the more advanced of the children's encyclopedias and the less difficult of the encyclopedias usually considered suitable for senior high schools.

Both the *Children's Catalog* and the *Standard Catalog for High School Libraries,* as well as the three American Library

Association booklists with titles beginning "A Basic Book Collection" [1] suggest titles of encyclopedias which are recommended for use in school libraries. These aids are especially helpful for selection of standard encyclopedias.

Before purchasing any set of reference books, especially when the title is new or not well-known, the librarian should check for recommendation in the *Booklist and Subscription Books Bulletin*. This was suggested in an earlier chapter but is emphasized again at this point. Administrators should also be made aware of the existence of this valuable publication and be urged never to purchase books in sets without asking the librarian to ascertain whether the *Bulletin* recommends them for use in school libraries. For reference books which are not evaluated in the *Booklist and Subscription Books Bulletin,* the section in each issue of the *Wilson Library Bulletin* known as "Current Reference Books" is helpful. This aid not only keeps the school librarian informed as to what new reference books are available but furnishes some evaluation as to their usefulness.

Where encyclopedias are kept up to date by what is known as continuous revision, that is revision of certain sections or addition of new topics with every printing, school librarians are advised to purchase a new set about every five years. It is the part of wisdom to stagger such purchases so that not more than one new edition of an encyclopedia will be purchased during the same school year. Since only about 10 per cent to 15 per cent of the annual budget in a school library can be allotted to the purchase of reference books, as is explained more fully in Chapter 6, the expediency of such advice is readily apparent.

Types of Reference Books Needed

In addition to encyclopedias, the school library collection should include dictionaries ranging from simple picture dictionaries for the very young children to unabridged dictionaries for senior high school use. At all levels, well-selected abridged dictionaries for ordinary information about words are helpful. In a

[1] See the list of book selection aids in the Appendix for full information.

high school which has courses in modern foreign languages, a dictionary for each language should be provided. At least one thesaurus will also be needed as well as other books useful in word study.

A practical suggestion for the use of dictionaries in the school library is to have one or two tables reserved for dictionaries and require pupils to use them there rather than to move the cumbersome dictionaries for use at various tables in the reading room. Each unabridged dictionary might then be kept on a revolving stand on the tables reserved for their use. The abridged dictionaries could be brought from and returned to the nearby reference shelves as needed. They will then be less liable to be left scattered about the room or carried away. Dictionary stands tend to limit the use of unabridged dictionaries which must be used while pupils stand.

Calls often come to the reference desk in the school library for information about people: authors of books which pupils are reading and on which they are preparing reports, people who are in the news, stars of the sports world, movies, and television. Biographical dictionaries of the *Who's Who* type for outstanding persons; the Kunitz-Haycraft authors series published by the H. W. Wilson Company (*Twentieth Century Authors* and its *Supplement* and the *Junior Book of Authors*) for authors and illustrators; and *Current Biography*, also published by the H. W. Wilson Company, for people in the news are essential to answer such demands.

Useful also in reference work are the yearbooks, or supplements by which encyclopedias are kept up to date. In addition, the reference librarian cannot well get along without such books as the *World Almanac* (New York World-Telegram and Sun), *Information Please Almanac* (Farrar, Straus and Cudahy), and Joseph N. Kane's *Famous First Facts* (H. W. Wilson Company, 1950). There are numerous handbooks, both of a literary and historical nature, that are convenient for a wide variety of questions. Maps, atlases, and gazetteers are essential in answering questions about the far-away places which have become more accessible and more important in this period of scientific and technological advance.

There is a need not only for indexes to materials on subjects, such as Eloise Rue's *Subject Index to Books for Primary Grades* (American Library Association, 1943) with its 1946 supplement and *Subject Index to Books for Intermediate Grades* (American Library Association, 1950) but also for indexes to various types of literature, such as fairy tales, poetry, plays, and short stories. Very important for reference work on current topics are the H. W. Wilson Company indexes, the *Readers' Guide to Periodical Literature* and the *Abridged Readers' Guide to Periodical Literature*, one of which, depending on the number of magazines subscribed to and kept for reference purposes, should be in every school library.

Selection of Reference Books

No attempt is made here to suggest all types of reference books needed in the school library or to compile a list of individual titles which should be in the reference collection of the school library. Though neither includes a special section devoted to reference books, both the *Standard Catalog for High School Libraries*, 7th edition, (H. W. Wilson Company, 1957) and the *Children's Catalog*, 9th edition, (H. W. Wilson Company, 1956) list books in various classes of the Dewey Decimal Classification which are valuable for the reference collection. Many are obviously of the type to be marked "R," placed in the reference collection, and used only in the library. A course in reference books and practice in doing reference work will help the school librarian decide what books will be most useful in the reference collection. For a wider choice of reference materials, the most practical guide for the school librarian is Louis Shores' *Basic Reference Sources* (American Library Association, 1954) though it contains many titles, of course, which are not suitable for school library work.

Other Reference Materials

Supplementing the actual reference collection are the many excellent books of non-fiction in the regular collection. A good reference librarian knows that any book with an index is a potential reference book, and the inclusion of an index is often the determining factor when a book is finally selected. Pupils should be taught early how to use an index and how to consult books from the general collection as well as those from the reference collection. This is especially important now that so many books in subject fields are available at all levels. While no one would suggest that there be a large proportion in the school library collection, an occasional textbook, different from that used in classrooms, is helpful in reference work.

To locate materials for reference, the card catalog should have a generous supply of subject entries. This refers not only to subject entries for entire books, but analytic subject entries to parts of books. In fact, analytic cards, both subject and title (referring to only a part of a book), are extremely useful in the card catalog of a school library. That is one reason for the insistence that the school librarian should not attempt to catalog the collection until after a course in cataloging has been taken. The smaller the collection the more necessary are indexes that open doors to every available bit of material. The librarian, and some teachers, will make use of indexes such as those mentioned earlier and the analytics in the *Children's Catalog* and *Standard Catalog for High School Libraries* but pupils expect to find, and rightly so, what they want through the card catalog. A card catalog is a good reference tool only if it is a real index to the contents of the books on the shelves. Every school library needs a good card catalog not only for reference work but for reading guidance demands as well.

Other sources of material for reference work are the vertical file and the picture collection. The vertical file, or information file, is particularly helpful for current topics so that a good daily paper should be clipped regularly for prompt filing. A good example of such material would be the first newspaper reports on the Russian Sputnik and the up-to-the-minute articles on outer space and guided missiles published following the Sputnik's launching on October 4, 1957. At first, these clippings constituted the library's only material on this current topic. Later, of course, magazine articles on the subject appeared. John Bryan Lewellen's *The Earth Satellite* (Knopf, 1957) written before the launching of the Sputnik and published soon afterwards has been followed by other books on this subject for the younger readers. At least one juvenile encyclopedia advertises the article on artificial satellites in its 1958 issue as an example of the up-to-dateness of the encyclopedia. Usually, after current topics have been covered in magazines and books, the vertical file material may prove less useful but it is a valuable reference for topics while they are still fresh.

The vertical file is usually the chief source of information on local history in the school library. Every available clipping on this subject should be preserved. Someone writes the history of the local town for the weekly newspaper. A historical building is torn down to make room for industry or is restored for posterity and, in either case, its history is recorded. The oldest resident of the community reminisces on his hundredth birthday. The school celebrates an anniversary at which time its history is recalled. Perhaps some of the older residents could be persuaded to recall and write down facts about the community. Nowhere in print, such material could be typed for the vertical file. All of this is grist for the mill when a teacher and his group of pupils decide, as they so often do, to explore the history of their own locality. Local history is only one example of material which the school library can supply largely from the vertical file.

The use of pictures in daily classroom activities has already been referred to in Chapter 3 on circulation. Often a reference question can best be answered from the picture collection. For example, a group is working on a mural to climax a unit on life in the Middle Ages and wants to know what type of shield a certain class of knight should carry. The drama class is staging one of Shakespeare's plays and needs information on how the heroine should wear her hair. The making of an Easter bunny is being held up until the elementary class can learn how the tail of a real rabbit is attached to its body. In such cases, the picture collection will provide the answers to pupils' questions.

Reference Questions

Several school librarians were requested to supply a list of questions presented to the reference desks in their libraries during a given week. Some of these questions are listed below to give an idea of the variety of questions asked in school libraries.

In two senior high schools, pupils wanted information on the following topics:

1. The five states of the Northwest Territory.
2. Biographies with settings before and after the Civil War.
3. The seven hills of Rome.
4. The death of Julius Caesar.
5. The second largest telescope in the world.
6. A picture of a cattle barge.
7. The type of window curtains used in the early passenger cars.
8. Juvenile delinquency.
9. Graphs depicting rise in the cost of living.
10. The meaning of Bar Mitzvah.
11. Dimensions of Columbus' three ships.
12. How to lead a panel discussion.
13. The date of the duel between Burr and Hamilton.
14. Picture of a theater in Shakespeare's day.
15. Majority necessary to pass an amendment to the Kentucky Constitution.
16. Present members of Eisenhower's cabinet.
17. The inscription on the monument at the Saratoga battlefield, which might explain why the bust of Benedict Arnold was omitted.

Two junior high schools presented a long list of questions from which the following were chosen:

1. Who was the first president who wore long pants?
2. What books for children has Jesse Stuart written?

3. Where can I find the story behind "The Star Spangled Banner"?
4. Have you a map showing the temperature zones of the United States?
5. Where can I find a book that shows Chinese lettering?
6. How is the date for Easter set?
7. Did James Whitcomb Riley write a poem about the Battle of Boonesborough?
8. Who were "Tokyo Rose" and "Axis Sally"?
9. Where can I find the standard of living in Kentucky?
10. How can sea water be made fit to drink?
11. Where is material about Henry Clay's home and the monument to him?
12. What kinds of guns were used in the War between the States?
13. When should a junior high school girl wear gloves?
14. What are the first-, second- and third-class cities of Kentucky?
15. What kind of sword was used in King Arthur's time?

Meanwhile, pupils in two elementary schools were bringing to the library their own private brand of reference problems as follows:

1. How to housebreak a cocker spaniel puppy; what to do for a sick parakeet; how to feed tropical fish; the kind of house needed to raise pigeons.
2. We found a leaf on the way to school and want to find what tree it came from. We are studying about the cave men and need to know about the caves they lived in.
3. Why don't people stand on their heads when the earth rotates? When people use solar heating for houses, what do they do when it is cloudy and rains?
4. How do bees stay alive when the flowers are all gone? Which of the wild animals hibernate in winter? Do other animals carry their babies in a pouch as the kangaroo does?
5. Is the man who wrote *Winnie the Pooh* dead? Where can I find something about who wrote *Mary Poppins*?

Practical Helps in Reference

A few practical suggestions may be offered to help the school librarian in the never-ending task of finding material to answer reference questions. It will pay to keep a record of questions asked. A long, narrow pad of paper kept at the reference desk is convenient for this purpose. The current date should be stamped at the top of each sheet. The question should be noted while the pupil is presenting his problem, or as soon thereafter as possible. When the same question is asked again, as it is certain to be if an entire class has been assigned to find the answer, a *score* may be marked at the right of the question instead of entering it again. As each question is answered, a *check* should be made at the left to indicate a completed transaction. The absence of a check mark signifies necessity for further search. If there is not time to list questions every day, this could be done at least sufficiently often enough to secure a sampling.

Such a record often is helpful in showing school administrators how the librarian spends his time. Furthermore, the proportion of questions answered will be an indication of the adequacy of the reference collection. On the other hand, unanswered questions may show up gaps in reference materials and lead to orders for materials to fill them. They are also a challenge to the librarian's ingenuity in finding the information.

Whenever locating the answer to a reference question is difficult and consumes more than the normal amount of time and effort, or when the answer is finally located in an unlikely source, the librarian would do well to make a record of the question and the source of the answer.

An example of such a question is that posed by a geometry teacher who assigned pupils to locate a geometrical theorem known as "The Bridge of Fools" with no indication as to whose theorem it was. The pupil first presenting the question to the librarian had already consulted the general encyclopedias without result. Because of its special section on "Mathematics," the *Lincoln Library of Essential Information* was consulted by librarian and pupil. The index included no entry under either "Bridge" or "Fools," though it did refer to a section under "Theorems" and there the desired theorem was located. Immediately, a card was made out and added to the file kept at the reference desk for questions difficult to locate (Figure 36). The next time "The

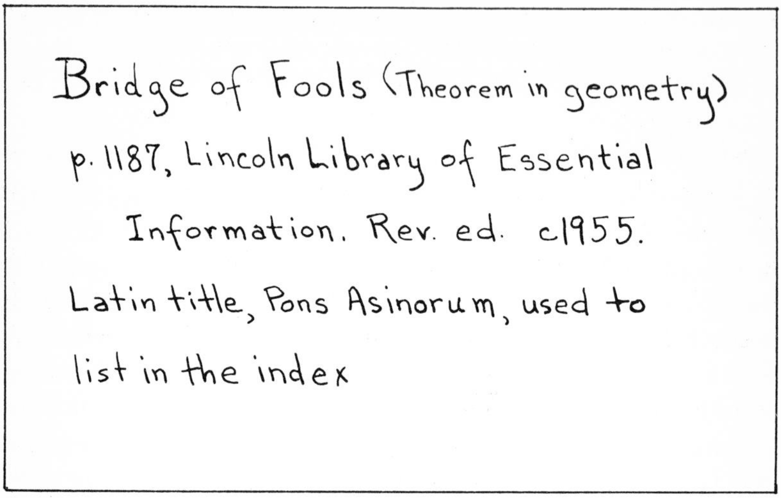

Bridge of Fools (Theorem in geometry)

p. 1187, Lincoln Library of Essential

Information. Rev. ed. c1955.

Latin title, Pons Asinorum, used to

list in the index

FIGURE 36
Card for file of reference sources difficult to locate

Bridge of Fools" was assigned, the librarian was ready with the answer. There are not many questions of this type but they can be knotty and, since no one can keep all sources in mind, this simple file is a great time-saver.

Similarly, when an unlikely source of information shows up in a book, an analytic should be added to the card catalog. An example of this arose when a teacher wanted information about Anne Carroll Moore. Being a writer of books about children's reading rather than of books for children, Miss Moore was not included in the *Junior Book of Authors*. The card catalog listed nothing about her and the school did not own the index *Library Literature*. The librarian remembered having seen a sketch of Anne Carroll Moore's life in some book for which analytics were not made at the time the book was cataloged because the persons included were not the usual ones about whom pupils ask. A search of the books in 920, Collective Biography, turned up an interesting sketch of Anne Carroll Moore's work as Chapter 3 of *Girls Who Did* (Dutton, 1927) by Helen Ferris and Virginia Moore. The book was laid aside and an analytic card made and filed in the card catalog, not only for Anne Carroll Moore but also for May Lamberton Becker, to whose work another chapter of the book was devoted.

Importance of Reference Work

There is no part of library service to schools more interesting than reference work. It keeps the librarian in close touch with the procedure of most classrooms and gives him an opportunity to work closely with pupils and teachers. The alert school librarian probably knows more intimately what goes on curriculum-wise in various classrooms than does the principal, concerned as he is with administrative duties. The librarian knows which grade is doing a unit on Eskimos and which is studying the topic of "Hot Lands." He can tell how far along the fifth grade is in the history of their state or what period in American history the tenth graders have reached. Throughout the school day he learns to shift quickly from Pony Express to modern communication; from democracy to communism; from prehistoric times to life in the Middle Ages; from space travel and man-made satellites to customs of ancient Rome; and from etiquette to juvenile delinquency. He becomes deeply interested in Leif the Lucky when he must find something on Louis Armstrong. He begins to feel at home in Alaska when a call comes and he is off to Pitcairn Island.

Reference work is probably the most important work which the school librarian does. It most closely identifies him with the entire school and its objectives and qualifies him as a full-fledged faculty member though he has no homeroom, makes no assignments, and grades no examination papers. While somebody else may stand in for the librarian at many other duties in the school library, he is the one who can best help pupils and teachers in making the fullest use of library materials. This service culminates in reference work, without which the library never functions to fullest capacity in the school of which it is a part.

Reference work is a satisfying experience and offers its own rewards. It helps the librarian keep abreast of the times. It furnishes an opportunity for using every bit of information he has previously acquired. "Nothing is ever lost" is certainly true at the reference desk where the librarian must know a little about everything. Any librarian knows the thrill of finding the answer, especially if the search proved not easy. He also knows the difficulty of finding answers to multitudinous questions on every conceivable subject. The work at the reference desk is probably the most appreciated. "Gee, thanks" from a pupil or a word of commendation from a teacher compensates the librarian for such services rendered.

The one drawback is that, with so many other duties which are also the librarian's responsibility, there is often not sufficient time for a really good job at the reference desk. Consequently, as mentioned in the section on reading guidance, the librarian sometimes feels a sense of frustration.

For this reason, school librarians and teachers should make every effort to teach pupils how to do simple reference work for themselves so that they will not have to refer every question to the librarian. Pupil assistants can help other pupils to locate encyclopedias and general reference books and to find materials in them and should call on the librarian only when the question seems too difficult for them. Teachers and librarians must work cooperatively in teaching pupils to be self-sufficient in using the library and its materials. It would help also if teachers would plan various questions for different pupils and not require each member of the class to find the answer to the same one. Too much time is consumed, for instance, when everybody in the class needs to find what makes the jumping bean jump, especially if only one source in the library yields the correct answer. The net result is that the librarian is kept on the jump.

Teaching the Use of the Library

The number one problem in the use of materials in all school libraries is that of training pupils to find things for themselves, generally spoken of as "teaching the use of the library." Yet it is true that the best use of materials results when pupils find as much as possible for themselves and refer to the librarian when questions lead to materials which they have not been able to locate. Teaching the use of the library thus becomes an important part of school library work which should be the joint responsibility of teachers and the librarian.

Very seldom are teachers and librarians agreed as to how the subject should be taught, or satisfied with the method used. The first problem that arises is: Who is to teach the use of the library? The teacher certainly knows his pupils and their needs and can most wisely determine the best time for each library skill to be presented. Yet the teacher is often not too well acquainted with library tools or with methods of explaining their use. Besides, the curriculum is usually so full that it is hard to make room for this additional subject, important as it is. The librarian certainly knows library materials and realizes fully their usefulness to classroom learning but he is somewhat removed from classroom procedure and cannot know all the pupils. As for time—whose daily schedule is already more crowded than that of the school librarian?

The next question is whether the use of the library should be taught in the classroom or in the library itself. If teaching takes place entirely in the classroom, the learning situation is removed from much material that cannot be made available outside the library. Yet, when the lessons are taught altogether in the library, it means that library materials are not generally available to other pupils while the course is in progress. In fact, it usually means that the library must be closed for the period to other pupils.

Third, how shall the use of the library be taught—as a separate unit or in connection with classroom subjects or units? Both the teachers and the librarian would agree that the latter is preferable. Yet, in general practice, the use of the library is largely taught as a separate group of lessons. To ascertain whether pupils have actually learned how to use library tools is another part of this problem. An identical exercise done by all and handed in hardly seems the answer. There is nothing to hinder pupils from copying, with skillful variations, the answers that have been looked up by the more enterprising, or dividing the task and pooling results to mutual benefit. Exercises tailored to fit the needs of individual pupils are too time-consuming to be practicable. A test may prove how much pupils have memorized without actually measuring skill in putting such information into practice when the pupil needs to use a book or the card catalog to locate it. All too often, in the face of such problems, teaching the use of the library is neglected or done in a rather haphazard manner. Notwithstanding these difficulties, however, many schools have developed good programs of teaching library use that have resulted in more adequate use of library materials. School librarians must assume responsibility, with the cooperation of teachers, for seeing that all pupils have instruction in this important phase of library work.

Topics to Be Covered

There seems to be general agreement as to what topics relating to library use need to be taught. They are roughly as follows:

1. Library regulations and procedures, such as circulation routines.
2. Parts of a book, especially with reference to how each may serve the reader, with emphasis on the index and its use.
3. Arrangement of books on the shelves, a brief account of the ten main classes of the Dewey Decimal Classification, and the letters used to indicate certain groups of books, such as biography, fiction, and short stories.
4. The card catalog as an index to books on the shelves and how to use it.
5. The use of dictionaries.
6. The use of encyclopedias, the types of information to be found in them, and the arrangement of different encyclopedias.
7. Other reference books in the collection: biographical dictionaries, historical handbooks, statistical abstracts, etc.

8. Periodical indexes as a key to material in current publications useful for reference purposes.
9. Other indexes, such as those to fairy tales, poetry, short stories, etc.
10. How to use atlases, globes, maps, and other geographical materials.
11. Types of materials in the picture collection and vertical file and how they may be used.
12. How to take usable notes on and outline material as read.
13. Simple form for making a bibliography of materials consulted.

The two last points have to do with using materials after they have been located; they are too often ignored in programs of teaching the use of the library.

A Proposed Teaching Program

A nearly ideal situation for teaching the use of the library in any school would be a program in which all teachers cooperated and the librarian served as coordinator. There would be a definite outline of topics to be presented in each grade of the elementary school, as there is for other school subjects. Additional material presented in junior high school would be built on what had been learned in the elementary grades, and high school topics would be based on what had been learned in junior high school. Each teacher would know library materials and how they may be used and each librarian would be familiar with the curriculum and understand classroom procedure. In the ideal physical arrangement of facilities, there would be a special classroom adjoining the library where classes could gather for lessons in the use of the library and to which library materials could be brought as needed. This room could also be available for the use of audio-visual materials, so that projectors and screen would not need to be moved to the classrooms. On occasion, the group studying the use of the library could be taken into the library itself for part or all of the lesson.

There would be an agreement in advance between the librarian and the teachers as to who should teach each topic. In general the teachers should teach the use of materials themselves and the librarian the actual use of the library. Any qualified teacher should be able to teach the parts of a book and their use, as well as the use of dictionaries and encyclopedias. Certainly, the reference materials of the various subject fields, such as literature, science, and social studies, should be so familiar to the teachers concerned that they could introduce pupils to the books and direct them in using such materials. As has been suggested earlier, but is emphasized here, a weak point in the use of library materials is that pupils often seem not to know what to do with them once the materials have been located. What school librarian has not observed pupils diligently copying or paraphrasing words from a reference book and wondered what the resulting report would be like? Pupils need much more help in learning how to read for various purposes, when to scan and when to study, how to take notes that are meaningful the next day, or to outline material as occasion demands. This part of teaching the use of the library is surely the responsibility of the teacher.

The librarian, on the other hand, is the best person to explain library procedures and to teach the Dewey Decimal Classification as related to the arrangement of books on the shelves, as well as the general arrangement of library materials. He should be responsible also for teaching the specialized library tools, such as the card catalog as an index to books on the shelves and periodical indexes as the key to current materials. The librarian also should help the pupils in developing a simple form for a bibliography. In brief, the librarian teaches pupils to locate materials; the teacher helps them to relate these materials to classroom activities. Close cooperation of teachers and the librarian is necessary in any program of teaching the use of the library.

Ideally, various aspects of the use of the library should be presented when pupils first have need for them. For example, a high school pupil will best profit from instruction on how to use the *Readers' Guide to Periodical Literature* the first time he needs to consult material in periodicals for a term paper. When he realizes how quickly and effectively he can find material on his given subject through the *Readers' Guide,* its usefulness is immediately clear to him and he will turn to it for other topics of a similar nature. Pupils on the elementary level will not fully comprehend the value of an index until they have learned how quickly they can locate a specific topic in any book by using the index.

The third-grade pupil may be introduced to the card catalog when he first needs to locate a book by a given title. The sixth grader goes into the study of the card catalog further when he is required to look for several books on the same subject. The senior in high school will be ready to study the parts of the catalog card that are useful in making a bibliography for a term paper. He will notice the form of the author's name, the title, followed by any sub-title or edition, the publisher and date. He will understand why paging is important as he uses only a part, or all, of the book being cited.

With this sort of program in teaching the use of the library, the student in college would need only to transfer his knowledge of use of the card catalog to a larger one. The high school graduate who does not attend college would have no difficulty in using even a large public library.

As suggested by the above, the best approach to teaching the use of the library is functional, rather than formal although the latter has long been common practice. The best demonstration of the functional approach is found in Chapters 1 to 4 of Martin Rossoff's manual, *Using Your High School Library* (H. W. Wilson Company, 1952). In these chapters are presented four units, typical of those used in any high school, as follows: A Topic in Biography: Bing Crosby; A Topic in Science: Guided Missiles; A Topic in Geography: India; and A Topic in Social Studies: Labor and Labor Unions. These or similar topics are studied by high school classes, are within the interests of high school pupils, and any good school library would have an assortment of materials on the subjects. The different reference tools are presented as being usful for a particular topic and would thus be more meaningful to the student. While topics would vary from grade to grade and school to school, the approach is educationally sound and would serve to integrate teaching the use of the library with the teaching of subject materials as it should be.

Another recent manual which should be helpful in this connection is *Integrating Library Instruction with Classroom Teaching at Plainview Junior High School,* by Elsa R. Berner (American Library Association, 1958).

Materials for Teaching the Use of the Library

One of the biggest contributions which the school library can make to the program of teaching the use of the library is that of furnishing materials for teaching. The librarian should be alert to gather materials and to make them available to teachers. Types of materials available for this purpose are:

1. Textual materials treating various phases of library use.[2]

   a. Full texts, such as those by Jessie Boyd and others on the high school level, and Mott and Baisden for elementary school use.

   b. Books on libraries that treat the use of the library among other topics, e.g., Walraven and Hall-Quest *Teaching Through the Elementary School Library* (H. W. Wilson Company, 1948, now o.p.)

   c. Textbooks which include suggested units of study on the use of the library such as those for teaching high school English.

   d. Manuals prepared for teaching the use of the library, e.g., *Using Your High School Library* by Rossoff, mentioned earlier.

2. Material on various phases of library use supplied by publishers.

   a. Sample pages of dictionaries, encyclopedias and periodical indexes.

   b. Pamphlets on how to use various reference books.

   c. Printed charts on the Dewey Decimal Classification, card catalog, periodical indexes, etc., for which there is a small charge.

   d. The H. W. Wilson Company's pamphlet, *How to Use the Readers' Guide* (free in quantities up to 50).

---

[2] A list of such materials will be found in the Appendix.

3. Set of charts, *Peabody Visual Aids*, available from Follett Library Book Company, Chicago, Ill.

4. Flash cards, contests, drills, games, etc. which may be prepared in the school. Many ideas are available from current issues of the *Wilson Library Bulletin* and from Fargo's *Activity Books.*[3]

5. Films, filmstrips, slides, etc. available on the use of the library.

6. Materials to be projected on the screen: sample catalog cards, title pages from books, and illustrations from books on the use of the library.

Teachers are more willing to accept responsibility for teaching the use of the library if they know teaching aids and materials are available.

Conclusion

While the school librarian must supervise all types of library duties, most of his time is spent working directly with pupils and their teachers. The three types of duties which consume the larger part of the librarian's school day are reading guidance, reference work, and teaching the use of the library. Reading guidance in the school library is important because the librarian has the opportunity to work with all pupils of school age with easy access to teachers and parents who can help in dealing with reading problems. In reference work the librarian endeavors to locate for pupils the less obvious materials to answer questions needed for classroom activities. It is also the librarian's responsibility to coordinate the program of teaching the use of the library and to provide as much material as possible for teachers and pupils. As in other phases of library work, the school librarian and teachers need to work closely together to assure the best possible library service for all the pupils.

[3] Lucile Foster Fargo, *Activity Book for School Libraries* (Chicago: American Library Association, 1938); *Activity Book Number Two, Library Projects for Children and Young People* (Chicago: American Library Association, 1945).

CHAPTER 5

KEEPING MATERIALS IN
GOOD CONDITION

Introduction

After materials begin to be used by and circulated to readers, the problem of wear and tear inevitably arises. Any materials that are used constantly, as they are sure to be in school libraries, will eventually wear out and need to be either repaired or discarded and probably replaced. This chapter considers the problems of wear and tear, methods for keeping materials in as good condition as possible, and the records needed when materials must finally be removed from the library collection. It also discusses binding and rebinding of materials and suggests simple methods for mending some materials in the library.

Shelving and Storage Space

One of the first steps in keeping materials in good condition is to provide adequate space for housing them. Every school library needs plenty of space to put things so that they may be kept in good order and be easily located on demand. This includes housing for materials both in the reading room and wherever storage is provided.

For books, it is necessary to provide adequate shelving. In an elementary school, this means shelving 5 feet high, providing five shelves and, in high school, shelves of 6 feet 10 inches to 7 feet in height, providing seven shelves. For books of standard dimensions, shelves may be 8 to 10 inches in depth, while reference books and other over-sized volumes require shelves 10 to 12 inches deep. The shelves themselves, regardless of other dimensions, should always be 3 feet in length between uprights. Longer shelves tend to sag when loaded with books; shorter shelves give a chopped-up look that detracts from the usually attractive appearance of books on the shelves.

In order to accommodate books that are either very tall or very small, shelves should be adjustable. This may be accomplished by having a perforated metal strip attached to each upright. Hooks at the end of the shelf will fit into the perforations. Or the shelf may rest on metal pins which have been screwed into holes drilled directly in the upright. The one exception to adjustable shelving is the section of picture book shelves mentioned in Chapter 2 for elementary school libraries. These shelves are provided with thin vertical partitions every 6 to 9 inches to keep large, flat picture books of varying sizes in an orderly, upright position. Picture book shelves need to be 10 to 12 inches in depth and the same in height between the shelves. They also should be placed low for use by very young children.

As stated earlier, books should always be shelved with their spines flush with the front edge of the shelf. Books should never be packed into the shelves so tightly that they may be damaged when they are pulled out. Care should also be taken that they are not torn by having a book end jammed into the pages. Nor should they be pushed back against the wall, especially if it has a rough finish. The lowest shelf should properly be tilted upward to make it easier to see the call numbers of the books placed on it.

Current magazines should be displayed on special sections with sloping shelves. Underneath these should be a flat shelf to house several back issues of each title, as suggested in Chapter 2. If magazines are arranged on the shelves in alphabetical order by title, it is easier to shelve and to locate them. There should be a notice on the shelf where each magazine would ordinarily be shelved to indicate those which may be found at the circulation desk. It was suggested in Chapter 3 that magazines which tend to disappear may need to be charged out to pupils who wish to use them during the day.

Reserved books, as stated earlier, should be shelved behind or near the circulation desk for easy supervision. The librarian, who does most of the reference work, should have the reference collection convenient to the desk which he uses when in the reading room. Material such as magazines and books on short-time loans which might prove tempting to readers, should not be placed near the exits.

One of the first duties assigned to pupil assistants is that of shelving books and reading the shelves. The latter process consists of examining shelves to make sure that all books are in their proper order. Assistants should be taught to read the entire shelf as each book is being shelved and to rearrange any books that are out of order. Periodically also, entire sections of shelves need to be read and arranged. This task is usually assigned to assistants in turn, both to prevent boredom and to make sure that all take part in the task. It cannot be emphasized too often that properly shelving books goes a long way to prevent them from receiving damage which may result later in the necessity for mending or rebinding.

Adequate shelving should also be provided in the space adjacent to the reading room: the librarian's office, work room, storage space and conference rooms. Shelves are always needed for new books in the process of preparation for use, duplicates, unbound magazines and materials waiting to be mended, rebound or discarded.

In the work room, cabinets should be provided on each side of and above the sink for the storage of library supplies, mending materials and many other things needed in a library. Some of the lower space should consist of large, flat drawers to store maps, charts, posters and the like. If shelves in the reading room must be used for supplies, cabinet doors should be provided for neater appearance. One ingenious school librarian solved this problem by installing a window shade to cover shelves housing supplies.

Picture collections and information file materials are housed in vertical files of legal size, four drawers in height. These should always have ball bearings so that the drawers will move in and out easily even when full.

Special housing units are available for various types of audiovisual materials and should be investigated by school libraries which have large quantities of such materials. The average library can probably house its audio-visual materials in shelves, cabinets or drawers provided for printed materials in the space adjacent to the reading room. Generally speaking, audio-visual materials need to be housed where pupils do not have open access to them and where it is possible at least to some extent to control heat and moisture.

Taking Inventory

Unless records of an inventory for the previous year are available it will be to the advantage of an incoming librarian to take inventory as early as possible in the fall semester. Otherwise, it will not be clear who is responsible if a heavy loss of books and other materials is revealed by an inventory at the end of the school year. School libraries should have an annual inventory, if possible, because, with so many teachers and pupils using materials and with many routines assigned largely to pupil assistants, some materials will inevitably be damaged or lost. The main purpose of the inventory is to ascertain whether needed materials are available and to provide replacements when they are no longer available.

Pupil assistants may be taught to take inventory with advice and supervision from the librarian. He will probably want to take over also the task of checking on materials reported missing and deciding on replacements. He will also make sure that the resulting records are accurate and clear. In an elementary school library, the librarian will have to do more of the actual work in inventory with pupils assisting, unless teachers are available for help.

Inventory should be taken at a time when the majority of books will be on the shelves and other materials largely in place. Where school librarians are employed for an extra month in the summer, this time might well be utilized for taking inventory after school closes or before it opens again in the fall. Many school librarians take inventory between semesters or during the last weeks of the school year. At either time books should be called into the library for inventory. It will also facilitate the process if shelves are read before inventory is taken.

Two persons will be required to take inventory, one to read the shelf list and the other to take books from the shelves and examine them, as an inventory should be used not only to ascertain whether materials are on hand but also to check on their condition. Because of the strain of the work, inventory should not be done by the same persons more than about two hours at a stretch and it is wise to shift positions at the end of the first hour, both to prevent lassitude and to give pupil assistants varied experience.

Because the shelf-list cards are filed in the same order in which the books stand on the shelves, the shelf list is used in taking inventory. One pupil assistant may be seated to read from the shelf-list drawer while the other stands at the shelves. As each shelf-list card is handled, the assistant reads the call number and the accession number listed on the shelf-list card, as follows:

398.2, 3363.
Pyle

The assistant at the shelf indicates that the book is on the shelf, removes the book, and checks to see that the call number on the spine and the call number and accession number on the book card and pocket correspond to those on the shelf-list card. Where there is a discrepancy, the book should not be returned to the shelf. The assistant at the shelf examines each book also for physical condition and, if the book needs mending or rebinding, a new card, or a new date-due slip or pocket, a slip in the pocket should indicate this, and the book should be laid aside. On this slip will also be noted any error in call number or accession number discovered in the examination. Thus it will not be necessary for another person to examine the book later to decide why it was laid aside in the first place.

When a book is not on the shelf, a paper clip or other signal should be attached to the corresponding shelf-list card. Some librarians advocate removing the rod and turning on end all cards for which books are not located on the shelf. This procedure is not recommended in the school library where pupil assistants take inventory because loose shelf-list cards might be removed and misplaced. In case more copies of the book than one are indicated on the shelf-list card, a light check in pencil should be placed beside the accession number of the book not found on the shelf. This may later be erased if the book is found.

After the books on the shelves have been checked with the shelf list, a penciled list of books not on the shelves should be made in the following form:

Call no.	Title	Acc. no.
398.2	Men of iron	3363
Pyle		

A separately written list is suggested as being easier to handle than the shelf list of clipped cards when searching for the missing books. Also the shelf list will then not need to be removed from its customary place where it is often needed when searching for any misplaced book.

As soon as this part of the inventory has been completed, the list of books not found on the shelves should be checked against the file for books still in circulation despite the request for their return, at the bindery, being mended in the work room, in storage, charged out in the special file for teachers, on reserve or in some special place for short-time loans, or in use for display or exhibit. If two collections (as for elementary and secondary readers) are housed in the same room, search for a missing book should be made on the shelves of both collections. Since the call number may be used in both collections, the distinguishing designation "J" or "H" might easily be overlooked and the book shelved in the wrong collection.

When each missing book is found, or the card for the book is somewhere in the circulation file indicating where the book is, a line should be drawn through its entry on the list of missing books. The clip should then be removed from the shelf-list card and any check beside the accession number erased. After all checking has been done, a final list of the books still unaccounted for in inventory should be typed. A copy should be kept at the desk, under glass if possible, so that assistants may watch out for the missing books in circulation where they often mysteriously make their appearance. Other copies of the list of missing books may be posted on the bulletin board in the library and other places in school where notices are customarily placed. Teachers and pupils should be asked to look for the books and homeroom representatives urged to help retrieve them. This is also an appropriate time to make a search of all school lockers, where books often lie forgotten.

After a waiting period of perhaps a month, during which some of the missing books have still not been located, a notation "Missing inventory 9/25/57" should be lettered lightly beside the accession number on the shelf-list card. If later the book is found, this notation may easily be erased and the book put back into circulation. During the prescribed waiting period, shelves should be checked occasionally just in case the book has been overlooked in circulation. For months afterward missing books will continue to be searched for by pupil assistants. A word of caution should be given to assistants taking inventory not to count as missing any book for which there is a previous notation beside the accession number on the shelf-list card which indicates the location or disposition of the book, such as missing in a previous inventory, in storage or the like.

Once in a while it becomes necessary to take inventory of a small collection which has not been cataloged or in any case not provided with a shelf list. In this case, a record on p-slips, one for each book on the shelves, should be made, using the same form as suggested for listing missing books. Slips should then be arranged in numerical order by the accession number and checked with the accession record. Those books on the accession record for which there are no slips are to be reported as missing. From then on, the process is the same as that described above, except that the p-slips are used for searching purposes instead of the list. Those p-slips should be kept until the books are cataloged so that "missing" can be recorded on the shelf-list cards for those titles still in the collection.

Weeding the Collection

Weeding is the process by which materials no longer useful are removed from the library collection. It is a definite part of and an inevitable result of taking inventory. However, weeding must also be carried on continuously if the library collection is to be kept fresh, alive and up to date. Types of materials which should be regularly weeded from the school library are those:

1. In such poor physical condition that the readers cannot use them or will receive the wrong idea about care of materials by doing so.

2. In which the print is too fine for reading in comfort.

3. Whose leaves have become yellowed and brittle with age. This is too often true of copies of the classics, a condition which discourages their use.

4. Which contain material that is out-dated or perhaps no longer true. This applies particularly to materials in science, or social studies, especially about other lands and peoples. The copyright date is a great help in evaluating this type of material, though not the only factor to be considered.

5. Which have been superseded by new and revised editions. On rare occasions a new edition of a book does not entirely supersede the previous edition, but usually it does.

6. Which are not suitable for the readers using the collection, as often happens in a library once serving secondary but now used by elementary school pupils, or vice versa. Unsuitable materials may also result from unsuitable gifts or mistakes in book selection.

7. Which are duplicates of books once popular but no longer used a great deal.

The task of weeding vertical file materials and picture collections is not so easily defined as that of weeding books. However, these materials should be gone through periodically to remove whatever is no longer valuable. Dating each piece of material as it is added to the vertical file, as suggested in Chapter 2, is helpful if no printed date of publication appears on it. Certain rapidly changing current topics, such as atomic energy, need to be weeded more frequently than more static ones. Pictures are often outdated by the clothes worn by persons in them. Dress can also quickly outdate films and film-strips, a factor which must be considered in the process of weeding materials.

After materials suggested for weeding have been removed from the shelves or files, final disposition must be decided on. Books in poor physical condition with fine print and/or yellow pages, and consequently of no value anywhere, should be destroyed so that they will not again find their way back to the shelves. Suitable material, books and magazines, should be examined for pictures or other useful materials before being destroyed. Old editions should be replaced by newer editions and discarded unless there is a special reason for retaining the old one. Outdated material in non-fiction may well be looked over also by teachers of the subject or grade who might find a need not apparent to the librarian. One should not cater too much, however, to the teacher who clings to material just because he has always used it. When the decision to remove material is made by the librarian and teacher working together, it should be destroyed. Material unsuitable to the collection may be offered to other libraries in the school system or to a neighboring public or college library if the material is adult in nature.

Discarding a Book

When a book is taken from the collection altogether, a notation such as "Discarded 9/25/57" should be made beside the accession number on the corresponding shelf-list card. In case another library accepts the book, the notation should read "Donated to public library 9/25/57." As soon as possible after a book is discarded, it should be decided whether the book needs to be replaced with another copy. This will depend on whether the title is still of use to the collection. It may well be that another more recent book will be of more value, or a new or revised edition of the same book may be needed.

If the book is to be replaced by another copy, a card is placed with those for the next order and the book is ordered just as if it were a new title. When the copy arrives, it is processed for use like any other book, except that in cataloging nothing needs to be done except to add the new accession number to the shelf-list card. Any new edition of a book is treated like a new title and needs to be cataloged fully. This rule would not apply to various editions of a work of fiction by different publishers. The content being unchanged, these books may be counted as copies.

Withdrawal

Discarding a book, as discussed above, means that the physical book is removed from the collection and disposed of. The process of withdrawal takes place, however, when the title itself is no longer to be retained as a part of the library collection. Withdrawal may take place whether or not the book itself has been discarded. The withdrawal process may be applied as well to a book that is missing or lost.

When it has been decided to withdraw a title, all cards for the book must be removed from the card catalog so that readers will not continue to ask for the book. The tracing on the author or main catalog card lists all added entries, that is, title card, subject cards, and analytics to parts of books, if any are used, and thus indicates which cards are to be removed from the catalog. Pupil assistants may be taught to remove cards and arrange them in sets for the librarian to check before they are destroyed.

The shelf-list card, being generally considered a permanent record, should be retained. Beside the accession number, notation should be made as "Withdrawn 9/25/57." [1] The card may be retained in the "live" shelf list or removed and filed with others of like nature behind a guide card marked "Withdrawn." The decision as to choice of method will probably depend on the number of cards for withdrawn books which the library has. Assistants must remember, however, to check both the live and withdrawn shelf lists when searching for a book, if the two sections are kept. Since space is a problem in a school library, the librarian may decide to discard shelf-list cards for withdrawn books after a stated period.

It is not recommended that notation as to the final disposition of a book be made also on the accession record. Since it must be

---

[1] For all notations suggested on shelf-list cards, reasonable abbreviations may be used. A list of these should be given in the circulation manual.

on the shelf list for taking inventory, notation on the accession
record would be a duplication. However, some school librarians
prefer to make notations in the accession book, rather than on the
shelf list, and seem to get along well with this method. When
taking inventory in libraries which put notations only on the
accession record, the list of missing books would need to be
checked with it. The shelf-list cards for discarded and withdrawn
books are not then retained. In the case of small collections
which have not yet been cataloged or, in any event have no shelf
list, notations would have to be made on the accession record.

Record of Book Collection

If the record of the collection is to be correct at the end of
the school year, a continuous record must be kept of additions to
and removals from the collection. As suggested earlier, a 3" by 5"
card may be kept in front of the shelf list on which is entered
the number of books added to the library in each division of the
Dewey Decimal Classification as they are cataloged. A similar
card may be kept there also for the record of books removed
from the collection (Figures 37 and 38). One school librarian
suggests that an easy way to keep count of books added is to put
the order cards for all books processed behind a guide card
marked "Books Added, 1957-58." The order cards are arranged
by classification numbers and a count may be taken at any time,
certainly when the record of the book collection is made. At the
end of the school year statistics from the cards showing additions
and losses, regardless of the reason, should be combined to compile a complete annual record of the book collection (Figure 39).
Since there is no accession record for materials in the vertical file
and picture collection, a record of the number of items in each
is not so essential. However, if a count is considered desirable,
it could be kept in the same manner as suggested for material
that has been cataloged, except for designation by classification.

Materials in Storage

Materials to be stored are considered separately since they
are handled somewhat differently from materials that are being

	1957-58
Books added to collection	Gift
000	
100	
200	
300	
400	
500	
600	
700	
800	
900	
B	
F	

FIGURE 37

Record of books added to collection

FIGURE 38

Record of books no longer in collection

Books removed			1957-58
	Lost or Missing	Discarded	Withdrawn
000			
100			
200			
300			
400			
500			
600			
700			
800			
900			
B			
F			

Record of Book Collection — A. B. C. School for Boys — Year

Class. No.	Number in Collection	Number added during year		Number removed from collection			Number in Collection
		Purchase	Gift	Lost or Missing	Discarded	Withdrawn	
000							
100							
200							
300							
400							
500							
600							
700							
800							
900							
B							
F							

FIGURE 39

Record of book collection

removed permanently.) Their temporary removal is most often forced by lack of shelf space in the reading room itself. Material subject to storage will be older books of non-fiction used very little; duplicates of books, several copies of which were purchased during the height of a popularity which has since waned; and seasonal materials used for only a brief period of time each year, such as Christmas or Easter. Often, after being stored for a while, some of these will be discarded and probably withdrawn. In either case, the above outlined routine for discarding or withdrawing should be followed.

Methods of Storage

Materials in a school library may be stored in any one of three ways. In the first place, the top row of shelves, too tall for pupils using the reading room, may be used for storage space, especially in the case of seasonal material. It will be preferable from the standpoint of appearances if these shelves can be provided with hinged covers of cork board which may be raised as materials are needed. The cork board also provides additional space for displaying book jackets or other materials, including colorful art work from classroom projects and units. As has been previously stated, any additional space provided adjacent to the library should be equipped with shelves wherever wall space permits. A separate room for storage, especially of back issues of unbound magazines, is highly desirable in school libraries. Here the height of shelves is not so important since a step stool or ladder may be employed to reach the very tall shelves. This space provides the second and most common means for storage. When all available shelves have been exhausted, materials must sometimes be packed into stout cartons and probably assigned space elsewhere—the third and least desirable method for storing materials.

Materials stored in the reading room itself should be as near as possible to other materials in the same classification so as to be easily accessible. The book cards will remain in the books and the shelf list will not be changed. But whenever material is stored outside the reading room, the book card should be removed and the current date stamped beside the notation as "Storage 9/25/57," indicating regular storage in the adjoining room, or "Storage-Box 11—9/25/57" when box storage is being used. Each carton should be plainly marked with the box number and its contents, as "Box 12—Non-fiction, 917-918" or "Box 16—Fiction,

A-C." If box storage is used for any extended period of time, the books should be inspected periodically for silverfish, and moth crystals sprinkled in the boxes to prevent them.

The notation suggested should also be penciled lightly on the shelf-list card beside the accession number of every book stored. Book cards for materials stored outside the reading room should be kept together in the circulation files behind a guide card marked "Storage," and should be consulted in any search for missing books, especially at the time of inventory.

Storing Unbound Magazines

For reference purposes school libraries generally, especially on the high school level, are advised to keep for three to five years the issues of those magazines subscribed for which are indexed in *Abridged Readers' Guide* or *Readers' Guide*, depending on the index used. Available space and potential demand will doubtless determine how many magazines the school library stores. Experience proves that it requires regular shelving around 250 square feet of floor space to house five years' issues of all magazines indexed in the *Abridged Readers' Guide*. This would be a room almost half as large as the average classroom, which is some indication of the storage problem in school libraries.

When magazines are no longer current, they are placed with other recent issues in the space provided in the magazine shelving section, as suggested in Chapter 2, according to the library policy. After this period has passed, the unbound numbers are retired to the storage room where they are kept flat on shelves 10 to 12 inches wide. As the volumes are completed, the magazines are grouped by volumes of 3 months, 6 months or the year, depending on frequency of issue and bulk. The volumes are arranged chronologically with the latest on the bottom, if magazines lie flat, or to the left if they stand upright on the shelves. Each volume is tied in a package with flat tape since round cord, when tied, tends to cut the pages. The spines of the issues comprising the volume should face the reader and against these spines should be placed a card with a hole near the top and the bottom, giving title of magazine, volume number, and dates covered. The card is held in place by passing the tape through the holes and *under* the card, thus leaving the lettering exposed for easy reading (Figure 40).

FIGURE 40
Unbound magazines kept for reference

Before magazines are tied into volumes, they should be examined for missing issues or for those too badly damaged for use. Replacement copies of these should be ordered from the publishers or, in the case of very old issues, from a dealer in back issues of magazines. The librarian or one of the pupil assistants should secure any issue requested from storage and replace it after use. Because unbound magazines are kept solely for reference purposes, it is not advised that pupils be allowed to take them merely for leisure reading, for which there was ample time while the issues were current.

Magazines that are not indexed and consequently of little value for reference work should be disposed of after they have been examined for potential material for the vertical file and picture collections. This applies equally to the indexed magazines being discarded after the three- to five-year period has passed. Some librarians have found it helpful to keep magazines no longer of other value to the library to offer pupils who frequently need pictures to illustrate booklets, posters, charts, etc. This is not only a service which teachers and pupils appreciate but a practice which saves the library's collection from being mutilated. Magazines not kept by the library and still sufficiently intact to be read might be offered at the end of the school year to pupils who have only limited reading materials in their homes.

Binding Magazines

School libraries do not generally bind magazines. However, there are probably a few magazine titles in any school library that continue to be useful for reference or other purposes beyond the three- to five-year period during which school libraries are advised to keep them. Over the years, single issues to be tied into volumes become worn and there is always the problem of loss, with only a slim chance of being able to replace issues. It is probably wise to bind such titles, expensive as the process is. The following paragraphs are, therefore, addressed to those who bind any magazines for school libraries.

Certified Binderies

Class A binderies are certified under standards for Class A binding which are set by a committee of the Library Binding Institute and approved by the Book Binding Committee of the Resources and Technical Services Division of the American Library Association. All binderies that wish to be certified must meet and maintain these standards. A list of certified binderies is printed on the back cover of each issue of *The Library Binder,* the official publication of the Library Binding Institute.

Selection of a Bindery

The school librarian should, of course, send binding only to a certified bindery. As in the selection of dealers from whom to purchase materials, advice should be sought from other librarians as to certified binderies in the area. An important factor to be considered, other things being equal, is the promptness of the bindery in returning materials. In a school library materials are in constant demand and cannot be out of the library very long. The choice of a bindery will also be influenced by its proximity and particularly whether it provides a "pick-up" service. Having a bindery representative call on the library at regular intervals, or on request, saves the time of packing materials and the trouble and expense of shipping them. Furthermore, it gives the librarian and the bindery representative an opportunity to talk over mutual problems and thus assure better bindery service for the library. Where delivery service is not available, there should be an understanding with the bindery as to how the materials are to be shipped and who bears the expense of transportation. The wishes of the bindery should be acceded to in the matter of how materials should be prepared and packed. A visit by the librarian to the bindery is helpful and makes for good public relations. Seeing the process of rebinding books also helps the school librarian to understand why it proves expensive.

Stripping Magazines for the Bindery

In most magazines there are several pages both in front and toward the back of each issue devoted to advertising. These should be removed, either in the library or in the bindery as agreed. The busy school librarian will probably prefer that the "stripping" be done at the bindery. An exception for retaining such pages would be made in the case of magazines in which other usable material appears in the advertising section and where for any reason advertisements might make the material more valuable, as for instance in fashion magazines or those of a mechanical nature where pictures in advertisements supplement the text. If the table of contents appears on the cover, this would need to be retained for binding.

The Bindery Slip

Printed bindery slips may be obtained from the bindery patronized by the library, and a slip should accompany each volume of a magazine submitted for binding. When the first volume of a title is bound, the librarian should decide what material is to be used and what color. Buckram is usually chosen for magazines and the choice of color should be such that bound magazines whose titles in alphabetical order will stand next to each other on the shelves will not be the same color. Directions should also be given on the bindery slip as to the lettering on the spine. The name of the library may be added at extra cost, though this is hardly necessary in a school library. A duplicate

of the bindery slip should be made and kept on file in the library
for consultation when the next volume is sent to be bound (Figure 41a). This is to insure that all volumes of the same magazine
will be bound uniformly. After the first volume has been bound,
the bindery will make a "rub-off" as a pattern for succeeding
volumes. If the librarian should be requested to furnish the rub-
off, this is accomplished by holding a thin, strong sheet of paper
over the spine and rubbing the surface with a soft lead pencil
until a duplicate of the lettering appears on the paper.

Preparing Magazines for the Bindery

When the issues that make up a volume are complete, they
should be examined for physical condition. Duplicate copies
should be ordered for those issues missing or too badly damaged
to be included in the bound volume. If a title-page and index
are furnished by the publishers, these should be secured and
placed in the front of each volume. The magazines should be
arranged in chronological order from top to bottom, so that they
will be bound in the correct order.

The completed bindery slip is attached to the first page with
a bit of paste so that it will not be overlooked when the volume
arrives at the bindery. If there is pick-up service, it will be sufficient to place the magazines, tied in volumes with flat tape, in a
stout box. Otherwise, they must be packed more securely in
strong cartons with plenty of paper, excelsior, or other packing
substance to hold them firmly in place during shipment. The
fastest cheap method of transportation should be used if the package must be shipped to the bindery; this is usually rail for long
hauls, ordinary trucking for short ones. An alphabetical list of
the magazines submitted in any shipment should be made, including title, volume number, and inclusive dates. One copy of the
list should accompany the shipment and another be kept in the
library for checking the return shipment.

Return of Magazines from the Bindery

When magazines are returned from the bindery, the volumes
are checked first with the copy of the shipping list, to see that all

STYLE

✓ Full Buckram
......Full Cloth
......Other (Specify)

Color No.......................
......Red
......Maroon
......Orange
......Green
......Blue
......Tan
✓ Brown
......Black
......Gray

OTHER DIRECTIONS

LETTERING FOR BACK
(Follow exactly wording and arrangement as given below)

Title — Author
Wilson Library
Bulletin

Series — Volume — Date
v. 32
1957-58

Call number

Name of library

GAYLORD NO. 2 PRINTED IN U. S. A.

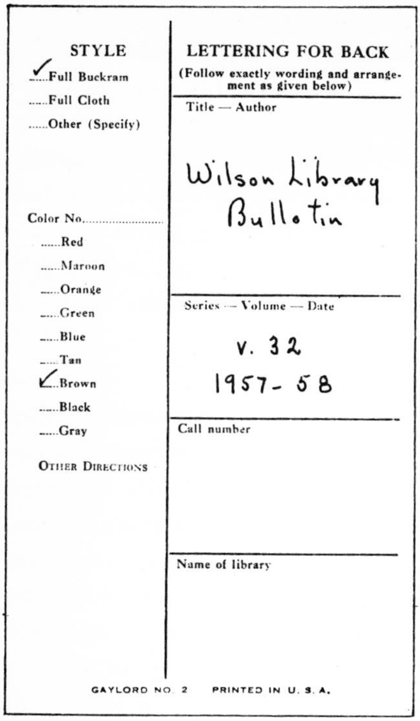

FIGURE 41a
Bindery slip for magazine

STYLE

......Full Buckram
✓ Full Cloth
......Other (Specify)

Color No.......................
......Red
......Maroon
......Orange
✓ Green
......Blue
......Tan
......Brown
......Black
......Gray

OTHER DIRECTIONS

LETTERING FOR BACK
(Follow exactly wording and arrangement as given below)

Title — Author
Little Women
Alcott

Series — Volume — Date

Call number
F
Alco

Name of library

GAYLORD NO. 2 PRINTED IN U. S. A.

FIGURE 41b
Bindery slip for book

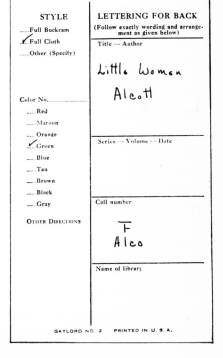

have been returned. If not, an invoice or accompanying letter from the bindery should explain the delay. The spine should be checked against the file of duplicate bindery slips to make sure the bindery has followed instructions for lettering. The volume is then collated to make sure that all issues and pages are present and in correct order. If there is an error, the volume should be returned to the bindery for correction as soon as possible.

Bound magazines are usually not cataloged in the school library but there should be a card in the shelf list for each title bound for the purpose of showing the library's holdings. Each volume is assigned an accession number as it is added to the collection and this number is noted on the shelf-list card. Bound magazines are placed on the shelves alphabetically by title.

Binding Costs

Prices charged by all certified binderies run about the same. Since prices for binding are determined by the height of the volume, magazine binding is costly. For that reason, school librarians are advised to bind only those titles that appear to have permanent value. They should also inquire of the binderies regarding the possibility of getting "flush" or storage binding, which costs about half as much as regular binding. In this type of binding the cover is usually of cardboard with cloth spine, the sewing is less durable, and the cover is flush with the pages, giving a flat rather than a rounded appearance. In school libraries where the use of bound magazines is limited, this type of binding should be sufficient. Also, in the manuals on mending mentioned later as being available from library supply houses, there are suggestions for applying plastic paste to the spines of several issues of a magazine to form a volume.

Rebinding Books

In Chapter 1 there was discussed the possibility of ordering prebound copies of books that will receive hard wear, especially for use in elementary schools. This practice will prevent having to rebind the books after only a few circulations or will at least postpone the need for rebinding. However, in any school library, many books are purchased in trade bindings which show wear after only brief use in circulation. Consequently, if the book is valuable to the collection, it will eventually have to be rebound.

A book to be rebound is first of all one that the library wishes to keep; otherwise, the book may be allowed just to wear out. The paper should be of good quality with enough rag content so that the sewing will hold without tearing the pages. This is often not true of pages in reprint editions. The margins of the pages should be sufficiently wide to allow trimming at the bindery. This is especially important as regards the inner margins, which should be at least half an inch wide. The print also should be sufficiently large and clear with appropriate leading for easy reading. A book with fine print should be replaced with a better edition rather than be rebound. All the pages should be present or else replaced in either typed or photostatic form before the book is rebound. If a book is to be rebound with one page missing, as might be possible in a large compilation of poetry, for example, attention should be called to this fact when the book is sent to the bindery. Otherwise, the book will be returned or the rebinding process delayed while the librarian is asked for instructions.

In sending books to the bindery, as in sending magazines, a binding slip may be made giving specific instructions (Figure 41b). But this is not really necessary and the school librarian will save time by giving only general instructions for all books. Very colorful books may be obtained simply by agreeing to accept any bright colors and an assortment of fabrics for rebound books. Wherever "picture covers" are available, these should be insisted upon for rebound books in school libraries. Picture covers are advertised in library periodicals under various trade names; they are bindings with an appropriate illustration from the book printed on the cover. Where such covers are not available, the bindery should be requested to use a variety of attractive designs now available for covers. There is really no longer any excuse for a plain black, blue or brown cover on a rebound book to be used by young readers. School librarians should insist that the covers of all rebound books be colorful and attractive, or change to a bindery which can supply such covers.

To save time of lettering in the library, the author, title, and call number should be stamped on the spine at the bindery. School librarians seem to prefer the stamping in white rather than gold because of legibility. Because mending is done as part of rebinding, the library should avoid anything but the simplest mending on books sent to be rebound. Rebinding no longer includes cleaning, however, and all books should be gone over with art gum or some other cleaning agent to remove dirty smudges either before they are sent to or when they are returned by the bindery.

When books are sent to the bindery, the book card must be removed from the pocket. The cards should be arranged alphabetically and held together with a rubber band. To save time of marking each card, "Bindery" is lettered on the first card and the date sent stamped beside it. In case more than one bindery is used, the name of the bindery should also be lettered on the card. The cards are filed behind a guide card marked "Bindery" while the books are away. Before this is done, the cards should be used in making a list, arranged alphabetically by authors, of books sent to the bindery. One copy of this list should accompany the shipment of books and another be kept on file in the school library. The books are then packed either to be picked up by the bindery truck or for shipment, according to instructions suggested for magazines.

Books Returned from the Bindery

When the rebound books are returned to the library, the shipment is checked against the list of books sent and the bindery is notified if any volumes are missing. The books should be collated and any not in good condition returned at once to the bindery for correction. It will of course be necessary to replace the date-due slip and book pocket, destroyed when the old binding was removed, after which the book card should be returned to the pocket. The accession number should be checked in each case.

This is also a convenient time to prepare new cards for books whose cards are filled up or nearly so, according to the instructions given in Chapter 3. It will not be necessary to shellac the spines of rebound books, unless lettering on the spine is done in the library.

The books are then ready to be placed on the shelves for circulation. Often rebinding makes the books look so much like new that their presence on the shelves has the same effect as new books in encouraging circulation. While rebinding is expensive, it does prolong the use of a book. In fact the cover of a rebound book often lasts longer than the pages inside.

Mending Books

Books in a school library are subjected to strenuous handling by young readers. Such treatment takes its toll of a book in dirty smudges on pages and covers, tears in the pages, corners turned down until they become dog-eared, pages that become loose and fall out, worn backstrip, and eventually the book's coming out of its cover. Books that are scheduled for rebinding, as already stated, should be mended as little as possible. But, apart from the books that are sent to the bindery, there are many useful books whose lives may be prolonged and usefulness extended by a few simple processes of cleaning, mending and recasing.

It should be emphasized that not all libraries should undertake an extensive book repairing program. The busy school librarian will certainly not take time from professional duties to repair books. There are often, however, pupils among the library assistants who with only minimum instruction are able to do a creditable job of book repairing. Or there may be someone in the community, perhaps a member of the Parent-Teacher Association, who will be able to offer both time and talent in making worn books look better and last longer. Suggested here are some simple processes that can be performed in any school library which will make books last longer or extend the time of circulation before rebinding them.

As explained in Chapter 3, assistants at the circulation desk should be instructed to examine for damages all materials as they are returned. If time permits, minor repairs may be made at the desk. Materials with more serious damages should be laid aside for repairs in the work room.

Mending Supplies

The following supplies will be needed for book repairs:

A jar of paste with plastic ingredients, available from any library supply house

A paste brush about an inch wide

A few thin round sticks for applying paste to small surfaces

A good pair of long, keen scissors

A book repair knife

A bone folder

An art gum and an ink eraser

A roll of waxed paper

A cake of Ivory soap

A package of margin papers

A box of facial tissues for removing excess paste

Double-stitched binding of various widths for recasing books and reinforcing magazines

Book cloth or recasing leather in rolls of various widths and colors for replacing back strips

Discarded newspapers to be placed on work tables and used for pasting surfaces

To Clean Books

Pencil marks and smudges of dirty fingers may be removed with art gum and elbow grease. Ink erasers should be used with care when the ink spot is on the printed page, lest the letters be eradicated with the ink. Some ink, including that used in ball-point pens, will not come off even with an ink eraser. No satisfactory method seems to have been found for removing crayon marks. Hence pupils should be warned against the use of crayons when handling books and advised to keep books where younger members of the family cannot get at them with crayons. Soiled covers may be improved by rubbing them with one of the following: (1) a sponge wrung out in wood alcohol or water to which vinegar has been added; (2) a slightly oily soft cloth; or (3) a very slightly damp cloth rubbed at frequent intervals on Ivory soap. The last method is especially effective on covers previously gone over with shellac.

To Mend Torn Pages

Recent developments in the pressure-sensitive mending tapes have produced several varieties which are specially designed for the repair of torn pages. A roll of this improved kind, available from library supply houses, should be equipment for every school library desk. Whenever a tear in a page is discovered, a piece of this tape large enough to cover the tear should be applied and pressed flat with the thumb. The tape is transparent and print can be easily read through it. The mend will appear less conspicuous if the tape is always applied to the back side of the page, the side away from the reader as he turns the pages.

Inexperienced librarians are here cautioned against using the ordinary variety of cellophane tape which has long been standard office equipment for repair work. The use of such tape leads to further damage to the book because the adhesive discolors, oozes at the corners, and tends to harden with age. The new type of tape tends to dry out so should not be ordered in large quantities and preferably in small rolls.

To Replace Loose Pages

A very simple procedure is that of replacing a single loose page. In this case, the inside edge of the loose page should be cleaned of particles. By means of a small brush, a little plastic paste is applied to a depth of not more than an eighth of an inch along the edge of the pages. The process here involved is the pasting of the loose page to the next page of the book. That is the reason for keeping the paste line narrow. Some menders prefer to apply paste only to the edge of the page so that it will ooze and adhere to the page on each side of the loose page. In either case the loose page is replaced in the book and pressed lightly into the groove.

The librarian will occasionally have the problem of a loose page which, because it has been torn out, is no longer the same width as the other pages of the book. Before re-inserting the page, it must be restored to its original width. The torn back edge should be trimmed. A strip of margin paper the length of the page should be pasted to it and trimmed to the proper width. Then the pasting process described above may be performed. Margin paper may be used also to repair the outer edges of the pages and to make a hinge for replacing plates or other heavy pages. In the absence of margin paper, strips of a good quality of rag bond may be used instead.

A sheet of waxed paper should always be placed over and under the page being repaired to keep paste from damaging neighboring pages. The user should be cautioned, however, that paste with plastic ingredients will adhere even to waxed paper if used to excess. It also is difficult if not impossible to remove from clothing. A weight should be placed on top of a book so that the pages will be kept flat while the paste is drying.

To Tighten a Book in Its Hinges

Probably the first place where wear on a book takes its toll is in the hinges which begin to loosen as soon as the book is circulated (Figure 42). If first aid is applied as soon as possible, it will defer, even prevent, the necessity for more complicated repairs.

As soon as it is noticed that a book is becoming loose in its hinges, the book should be placed upright to allow the hinge to spread. With a thin round stick obtained from library supply houses (a knitting needle will serve as well) a small amount of paste with plastic ingredients should be applied to the inside of each hinge. This is accomplished by inserting the stick under the loosened area and rolling the stick as it is removed to insure a smooth spreading of paste. Then the book is turned upside down and the process repeated on the other hinges. Assistants should

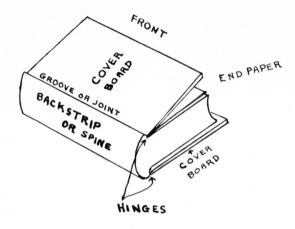

FIGURE 42
Parts of a book

be warned against the use of too much paste in the hinges for this
may make the backstrip too tight. The book is then closed and
laid flat while a bone folder is used to press each hinge into
place. After the paste has been allowed to dry, the book will
again be tight in its hinges.

Sometimes a book has been allowed to become so loose in its
hinges that the end papers have also pulled away from the front
and/or back covers. The same process may be used to repaste the
end papers to the cover boards and the book kept under pressure
until the paste is set. A piece of board the length of the book
should be placed over the cover against the groove of the book
(board should not cover hinges) and a hand clamp applied. In
the absence of a clamp, weight may be supplied by placing one
book upon another, making sure that hinges are not pressed.

This pasting process may be repeated as often as the loose
condition appears, though with paste containing plastic ingredients
one application will probably suffice. It should be emphasized
that the earlier this process is done, the better.

To Recase a Book

Often, through prolonged rough handling, a book may reach
the point where the entire cover has worked loose from the body.

The earlier stage of repair, involving repasting of the hinges and/ or end papers, is no longer adequate: it is necessary to recase the book. (Recasing is a simple mending process in which the body of the book is removed from its covers and reinforced with fresh backing material, after which the covers are replaced.)

The first step in recasing is to detach the body of the book from the cover. In order to do this a book repair knife or a pair of scissors is a necessary tool. The book is opened first at the front and then at the back, and the knife or scissors is used to slit through the groove which joins the end sheet to the cover board. Care must be exercised not to make an inadvertent cut in the cover material. (It may now be seen that the body of the book is composed of a number of sheaves of pages, or signatures, which have been firmly sewed together. This is the foundation of the spine.) Across the spine is glued the backing material or "super," a stiffened mesh fabric which reinforces the spine. (Figure 43). In case this material has deteriorated, it should be removed but care must be taken not to tear the stitches holding the signatures together. Crumbs of dried paste and shreds of old

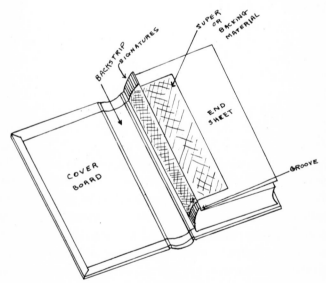

FIGURE 43
Body of book detached from cover

backing material should also be trimmed away. If the signatures have separated, as they often do especially at the top and bottom of the spine, paste containing plastic ingredients should be stippled over them to hold them together again. Paste may also be applied to the front and back end papers to insure a firm bond to the body of the book.

School librarians have found that double-stitched binding, secured from library supply houses, is an easily manipulated super to replace the book in its cover. Double-stitched binding is a double thickness of stiffened fabric held together by two rows of stitching. The distance between the rows varies so that it is possible to choose a width which exactly fits the spine of the book. The double set of tabs formed by the material left on the outside of each row of stitching are the means by which the body of the book is pasted into its cover. Double-stitched binding should be chosen of the proper width between rows of stitching to fit the spine. The piece should be cut about a quarter of an inch shorter than the book and the corners rounded slightly. This not only makes a neater finish but discourages pupils from picking at the corners.

A thin coat of paste should be applied to one side of the binding in the area between the two rows of stitching and is then pressed firmly against the spine of the book. The loose tabs of the double-stitched binding should be pasted to the end papers of the book and paste removed where in excess or added where dryness prevents adhesion. Paste is then applied to the other side of the double-stitched binding and the book placed carefully back into its covers, making sure it is right side up. The remaining set of loose tabs of the double-stitched binding are pasted down on each side of the cover boards and excess paste removed, or paste added as needed. Some librarians recommend the addition of new end papers in recasing a book but the busy school librarian and her helpers will hardly have time for this process. Usually the end papers are re-usable after reinforcement by plastic paste and the double-stitched binding is not unattractive in appearance.

The book should then be closed, making adjustments to fit the cover properly and the grooves of the hinges pressed with the bone folder. (Figure 42). The book should be placed under weights as described above until the paste has dried.

To Replace a Backstrip

Sometimes when a book has been too often pulled out from its place on the shelf by hooking the index finger over the top of the backstrip, the backstrip becomes worn. It often wears entirely off or so nearly so that it should be removed before some reader hastens the process. In case the sewing is still intact, the spine firm, and the super in good condition, a new backstrip may be added.

The worn backstrip may be sliced through at the hinges to remove it. Extreme care should be exercised not to cut through the super beneath, as this holds the front and back cover boards to the body of the book. Frayed threads should be trimmed off and any particles of dried paste removed.

A new backstrip should be cut about three inches wider than the thickness of the book so that there will be an overlap on to each cover board. The backstrip should also be about an inch and a half longer than the book itself to allow for a fold at the top and bottom. If book cloth is used for the backstrip, it should be torn to the desired size, and the frayed edges trimmed with the scissors.

Paste should then applied to the under side of the new back-strip material about an inch and a half from either edge. The backstrip is then applied over the spine and pasted to the cover by these overlaps, the area of the spine itself remaining free from paste. The effect is that of a quarter-binding with the new material forming the backstrip differing from that on the cover boards but overlapping part of the cover. In applying the back-strip to the book, the overlaps should be of equal width and the same amount allowed to protrude at top and bottom. As the backstrip is pressed against the cover until it adheres, excess paste should be removed.

Holding the book in one hand, the backstrip should be split at each hinge almost to the book's cover at top and bottom. The outside strips are folded over on to the inside cover and pressed firmly, more paste being added where needed. Then the two middle portions of the protruding backstrip are folded toward the spine and worked down until they are even with the book cover. Some librarians like to lift the end papers on the inside cover to insert the part of the backstrip folded over but here again the school librarian may not find time for this process though it does make a neater finish. With the book closed, a new groove is made by pressing the bone folder along the inside edge of the cover board on the front and the back of the book.

After the book has dried under weight, as previously suggested, the author, title, and call number should be lettered and the backstrip shellacked, as suggested for new books, before the mended book is again put into circulation.

To Mend Other Materials

Processes suggested for cleaning and mending books may be applied to other materials of paper and print. Mending films and filmstrips presents problems other than those described here. Double-stitched binding may be used to reinforce magazines and pamphlets that are not placed in pamphlet binders. To accomplish this, the materials are carefully removed from their covers and replaced in the same way as suggested for recasing books. The process is especially effective when the magazine or pamphlet has a flat spine and the signatures are stapled through from cover to cover. In the case of thin magazines or pamphlets which are stapled through the center, these may be further reinforced by a row of sewing applied while each is opened flat. This process is suggested also for pamphlets pasted into pamphlet covers by the inside overlaps. Otherwise the inside of the pamphlet may drop out with use leaving pages attached to flaps. Stitches on the spine may be covered over by a backstrip of Mystik tape for a neater finish outside.

Mending Manuals

For detailed information about mending or for instruction in various types of mending, the librarian is advised to secure a copy of one of the mending manuals prepared by and available from library supply houses. Demco of Madison, Wisconsin, and New Haven, Connecticut; Gaylord Brothers, Syracuse, New York, and Stockton, California; and Library Bureau of Remington Rand with offices in most major cities are among the library supply houses of long standing. These companies also have representatives who are available for group demonstrations of book repairing. There are also other library supply houses.

A very attractive book on book repairing is *Mending Books is Fun* by Brooke Byrne of the staff of the Lynn, Massachusetts, Public Library. (Minneapolis, Burgess Publishing Company, 1956). This book contains a great deal of practical information on keeping books in good condition, though the facetious manner in which it is written may detract from its appeal for some readers.

Teaching Care of Materials

Pupils need to be taught the proper use and care of library materials from the first time they are allowed to handle books. This instruction includes such simple things as having clean hands before looking at books, turning pages by the edges with dry fingers, using a book mark instead of folding down the corner of a page, never laying a book face down or forcing it open by pushing the covers back toward each other, and putting the book out of reach of younger children in the home. Later, readers may be taught to open a book properly, to cut pages with a letter opener when found uncut and be shown how books are made so that they will understand why they wear so quickly. Pupils should be urged to report any damage noted in books borrowed from the library as they return them so that steps may be taken to remedy the damage.

School librarians also need to make every effort to instill in the pupils a spirit which will discourage the practice of mutilating or taking materials from the library without permission. This practice may take the form of removing a portion of newspaper, magazine, or book with knife or scissors. It includes the habit which some pupils develop of drawing or writing on library materials. It may be as serious as the removal, one volume at a time, of the library's newest set of encyclopedias. Losses are a constantly recurring problem, no matter what precautions are taken against them. It takes cooperation on the part of the school librarian, his assistants, the teachers, and the administration to keep library losses to a minimum.

Conclusion

Keeping library materials in good condition starts with the proper shelving and filing of all types of materials. "A place for everything and everything in its place" is an excellent slogan for the school library. Materials in circulation should be watched constantly for damages that should be repaired before the materials are circulated again. Minor damages may often be mended at the circulation desk so that the material may be immediately returned to use. More extensive damages to materials may cause them to be laid aside until there is time for mending in the work room. Very little mending should be done when books are to be rebound.

Books that are of continuing value to the school library collection should be considered for rebinding at a Class A bindery. The school library will probably bind no magazines, or at least only a few. Indexed periodicals useful for reference purposes should be kept by volumes in good order so that they may be easily available for use on demand.

The annual inventory advised for school libraries will indicate what books are missing from the collection. Handling all the books at inventory time offers excellent opportunity for weeding, a process that actually goes on all the time. Materials no longer useful to the library should be discarded and, where the title is not to be retained, the book should be withdrawn and its cards removed from the card catalog.

Pupils should be taught the proper use of books and encouraged to take care of all materials as a means of prolonging their usefulness in the school.

CHAPTER 6

SCHOOL LIBRARY FINANCES

Introduction

Chapter 1 stated that financial support of school libraries, suggested as being essential for ordering books and supplies, would be discussed later. The present chapter discusses sources of support for school libraries, the school library appropriation, and the items to be covered by it, the advisability of a school library budget, with some suggestions for making one, and the records needed for keeping school library finances in order.

School Library Support

The chief source for the support of any school library is an appropriation from the local board of education. Most states also provide state aid for school libraries. One plan, still used in many states, involves some form of matching, on the county and/or state level, funds provided by the local school. A more recent trend is for the state to provide funds which will insure minimum standards of library service for all schools, and for the local board to supply additional funds for expansion of library services.

Often school libraries, especially on the elementary level, receive additional funds from local organizations, usually the Parent-Teacher Association. These funds, however, should be considered as supplementary rather than as the main support for the library program. It is also fairly common practice for the money collected in fines to be used by the school library as a contingent fund, as explained later in this chapter.

Standards for School Libraries

The school library appropriation is based on standards set by state departments of education, by accrediting agencies in the six regional associations, and for the nation by the American Library

Association. These standards vary widely and often prove confusing to administrators—and librarians—who attempt to meet them. For high schools attaining accreditation by the Southern Association of Colleges and Secondary Schools, the per pupil requirement for the support of school libraries is $1.25 for each of the first 500 enrolled, $1.00 per pupil for 500 to 1,000, and 75 cents for each pupil above 1,000. (At present there are no standards for accreditation of elementary schools by the Southern Association.) On the other hand, the national standard as set forth in *School Libraries for Today and Tomorrow* (American Library Association, 1945) suggests $1.50 per pupil for school libraries. More than a dozen years of inflation have, to be sure, made this figure inadequate; it should be nearer $2.00 or $2.50.

New standards for the nation's school libraries are now in preparation and are scheduled for publication by the American Library Association in 1959. The proposed standards were discussed at sessions of the American Association of School Libraries during the seventy-seventh annual conference of the American Library Association in San Francisco, in July 1958. School librarians are urged to acquaint themselves with these standards, including that of appropriations as soon as they are available.

Appropriations for School Library Services

In *School Library Standards*,[1] a digest of standards by states shows appropriations per pupil in high school libraries ranging from $2.50 in California and Kansas, and $2.00 in North Dakota and the state of Washington, to the figures of $1.50, $1.25 and $1.00 in many other states.

At the time the above-mentioned study was made, only twenty states had set up standards for elementary school libraries. The digest of these standards shows a per pupil appropriation of $2.50 in Minnesota, $2.00 in the state of Washington and $1.50 in Wisconsin. More common, however, are appropriations ranging from 50 cents to $1.00 per pupil.

[1] Nora E. Beust, *School Library Standards*, Bulletin 1954, no. 15 (Washington, D.C.: United States Department of Health, Education and Welfare, 1954)

By way of summary regarding appropriations for secondary schools, the study has this to say:

Nineteen States require expenditures ranging from 50 cents to $2.50 per pupil regardless of enrollment, and of these States 7 require additional funds for encyclopedias and other materials. Twelve States require a per pupil appropriation that ranges from 50 cents to $2.50, according to the size of the school.[2]

Expenditures for School Libraries

"Statistics of Public-School Libraries, 1953-54," released in October, 1957, as Chapter 6 of the *Biennial Survey of Education in the United States: 1953-54,* reports the average expenditure per pupil for library materials in the 128,831 schools included in the survey as $1.05.[3] This average was based on figures extending from 77 cents in Group I cities (100,000 or more population) to $1.42 in Group II cities (2,500 to 4,999). As anybody connected with school libraries realizes, $1.05 per pupil is not sufficient to meet the many present-day demands on the school library collection. A figure closer to $2.00 would be more nearly adequate. The deplorable fact is that in many school libraries the expenditure for school library service is far below this average. Furthermore, "eighty-three per cent of the elementary schools and seven per cent of the high schools have no school libraries," and thus make no expenditure for library service regardless of existing standards.

From a practical standpoint, a school librarian should make every effort to assure a definite appropriation for the library in line with standards governing his school and a definite expenditure of such funds for library service once they have been appropriated. There have been instances where money appropriated for the school library has been used for other purposes. Again it should be emphasized, as in Chapter 1, that it is the responsibility of the local school board and administration to see that the library is adequately supported.

[2] *Ibid.,* p. 6
[3] *Biennial Survey of Education in the United States: 1953-54* (Washington, D.C.: United States Government Printing Office, 1957) p. 29

Coverage of the School Library Appropriation

Regardless of what amount is appropriated for the school library, it should be expended only for library materials and their maintenance. The school library is furnished by the school with quarters, equipment, heat, light and water (when available in the library), janitor service and general school supplies. The salaries of the school librarian and any paid assistants are furnished also by the school except in rare cases where there is an arrangement between the school board and the public library for joint support of the school library. Consequently, the school library appropriation is expected to cover only expenditures for books and pamphlets, magazines and newspapers, materials for the vertical file and picture collection, plus maintenance through mending and binding. In most instances supplies that are definitely of a library nature (book cards and pockets, printed and plain catalog cards, etc.) are also included in the library budget. The present average library appropriation cannot be expected to cover audio-visual materials too.

With the fairly recent, but fast-growing, tendency for the school library to be designated as a materials center, where all types of instructional materials are housed, it is suggested that in schools where extensive audio-visual materials are purchased by and maintained in the school library, there should be additional funds for their support. There should also be additional staff to operate the expanded services of the school library which handles audio-visual as well as printed materials.

The School Library Budget

The school librarian will find it the part of wisdom to adopt an annual budget for the expenditure of the appropriation. Even though changing conditions during the school year may prevent following the budget to the letter, it will provide something at which to aim. The school library budget should be planned by the librarian, in consultation with teachers, and with approval of the principal. Many school libraries have a faculty library committee to work with the librarian in planning the budget and making other decisions concerning library services. Copies of the proposed budget should be made available to the various departments, or, in schools which are not set up by departments, to individual teachers in order that all may understand how the money appropriated is to be expended. At the same time, all the teachers should be urged to assume responsibility for submitting requests for needed materials in their special fields. There should be simple financial records that at any time will show those interested how much has been spent and how much still remains in the budget.

All funds should be encumbered (orders sent in to spend the appropriation) well before the close of school so that funds may be spent prior to the end of the fiscal year, usually June 30. Otherwise, unspent funds will revert to the general fund and no longer be available for library use. The school librarian should keep close watch on the budget and, in case any department toward the end of the school year has not sent in requests for materials equal to the amount allotted in the budget, advise the teachers to submit further requests. If the funds allotted are not actually needed for that department, the librarian should assure that such funds are used to fill gaps in the collection, or to purchase materials not otherwise covered by the budget. These funds might even be allotted to another department whose needs have not been met by its assigned portion of the budget. Such a shift of funds will probably affect budget making for the coming year, with a somewhat lower amount for the department failing to utilize its allotted funds. However, this failure on the part of any department to use its funds is not likely to happen where the budget is a cooperative venture, both in planning and in execution.

Because so many factors are involved, it is difficult to tell anyone precisely how to set up a school library budget. The budget varies from school library to school library as the library itself varies from school to school. It is possible, nevertheless, to lay down a few basic suggestions which may prove helpful in budget planning.

Authorities are seemingly agreed on very few areas of the budget for which definite percentages of the appropriation are suggested. For a number of years it has been suggested that from 10 to 15 per cent of the total budget be reserved for building the reference collection. This is not a large proportion, to be sure, and the fund is often used up in the purchase of one encyclopedia. For this reason, some small libraries arrange with the school administrators to pay for such expensive items as encyclopedias over a period of several years, rather than from one annual budget. In fact, several states, as shown by the digest of standards in *School Library Standards, 1954*, to which reference has already been made, specify that there must be funds above the per pupil appropriation for the purchase of encyclopedias. Such extra funds will certainly be needed if school libraries are to purchase revised editions of encyclopedias every five years, as is now required in some states and recommended for all school libraries.

For some years, the generally accepted standard has also called for an expenditure of 10 to 15 per cent of the budget for subscriptions to newspapers and magazines. No hard and fast rule can be applied here, however, because school libraries vary in the use made of magazines and consequently in the number needed. Furthermore, a smaller proportion of the budget would be needed for newspapers and magazines in elementary school libraries than in high school libraries, where greater use is made of magazines for reference purposes. School library standards for Minnesota, for instance, specify that 25 cents per pupil, with a minimum of $40.00, shall be spent for periodicals in both elementary and high school libraries. This may indicate a new trend in the proportion of the appropriation reserved for periodicals in the school library budget.

Pointers in Planning the Budget for Materials

In planning the school library budget for books and pamphlets treated as books, consideration should first be given to the present collection. Adequate records of the book collection, suggested in Chapter 5, will quickly show the number of the individual library's holdings in each decimal class. Otherwise, such information is quickly available from the shelf list, which also offers help as to the types of books in the collection and gives some idea of their recency. The school librarian needs to know in what fields his collection is strong and where it needs to be built up. The librarian must know his collection thoroughly; the only way is to study it.

Despite attempts to do so, no satisfactory formula for the relative proportions of the school library collection allotted to the various classes of the Dewey Decimal Classification has been worked out. Nor is this really practicable since school libraries vary with the schools they serve. Nevertheless, standard book selection aids, such as the *Children's Catalog* and the *Standard Catalog for High School Libraries,* as well as *A Basic Book Collection for Elementary Grades, A Basic Book Collection for Junior High Schools* and *A Basic Book Collection for High Schools* offer some guidance as to relative proportions among the various classes.

The school curriculum must also be taken into consideration: what subjects are taught, any particular stress or emphasis, and which departments make the most use of the library. Whenever new courses are added or old courses dropped, the library budget should be adjusted to meet these changes. The addition of courses in art will of necessity stress books in the 700's, while the installation of a commercial department will call for books on business English, secretarial practice and the like. Sometimes a shift of emphasis in the manner in which a course is taught will affect the types of materials needed. This often happens when a new teacher joins the faculty and is not satisfied with the materials selected by his predecessor.

The availability of materials in various fields is likewise a factor to be considered in budget allocations. A good example is found on the elementary level. Ten to fifteen years ago library collections in elementary schools consisted largely of picture books, fiction and folklore with some scattered titles in the various classes of non-fiction. This was due to the fact that there was a scarcity of materials in the non-fiction group on the elementary level. Now, however, there are new, colorful and interestingly written books for younger readers in every field and on practically every subject. Any elementary school librarian realizes this as he tries to keep up with the new writers and their works or to chart a course among all the "First books," "Real books," and "True books," not to mention the "All about books" and those the titles of which begin with "Let's," "What?" and "You and." The library budget of the elementary school will reflect this trend in the increased number of subject areas to be covered by the appropriation. There are also materials available on newer topics for use by high school pupils, especially in the physical and social sciences, which must be considered in budget planning.

The availability of library materials from other sources also enters into the picture. If, for instance, there is a good public library in the community or a well-stocked bookmobile makes regular and frequent stops at the school, the school library can then concentrate more exclusively on materials constantly needed in the school, depending on other collections for supplementary materials.

The high school library budget may be set up either by school departments or by divisions of the Dewey Decimal Classification. Choice of the latter plan does not signify, however, that the library will need to buy materials in each Dewey class. In any school library there would be need for only a few books in the 400's, though the need would be heavy in the 300's, 500's and 900's.

In the former case, where the budget is set up by departments, a problem arises over how to provide for fiction, biography, and other materials of a more or less recreational nature. English classes make considerable use of fiction, especially of a literary nature; yet it hardly seems fair to charge all fiction to the English department. Some fiction, especially that with a historical background, is used by the history department. Biography, of course, will be used by classes in English, history, science and perhaps other departments. To avoid complicated bookkeeping, it is perhaps wise in a budget set up by departments to have a fund for recreational material, including fiction and biography. In case the budget is set up by the Dewey Decimal Classification, biography would be included with the 900's and there would be a separate fund for fiction.

Since there are no departments in elementary schools, their budgets may be set up by the Dewey Decimal Classification, or better, by areas of instruction, such as social studies, science, etc. A separate amount would probably be allotted for folk literature, or this could be included in the fund for recreational material, which will also include fiction. If the Dewey Decimal Classification is used, a larger proportion would probably need to be allotted to the 300's, not only because of the various subjects allied with the curriculum, but also because that class includes folk literature. Another special area would include the picture books and easy books which serve the first three grades. Since practically all materials at any level are used by readers from as many as three grades, it does not seem advisable ever to set up the elementary school library budget by grades. Nor should materials in the elementary school library be separated or even designated by grades because this practice discourages browsing and selection to suit individual needs.

Budget for Non-Book Materials

A small part of the appropriation should be set aside for materials to build up the vertical file and picture collection— small because these materials are relatively inexpensive, often secured without cost. As suggested earlier, pamphlets ordered and otherwise treated as books, including cataloging, should be purchased from funds allotted to books in the category where the pamphlets belong.

If film strips or recordings are purchased in limited quantity by the school library, this part of the budget might be slightly higher to cover these as well as materials for the vertical file and picture collection under the general heading of "Non-book materials." It should again be emphasized, however, that the present

appropriations for school libraries *cannot* be expected to cover
extensive audio-visual materials. Instead, additional funds should
be appropriated for their purchase.

Supplies in the Library Budget

The annual budget for supplies varies in accordance with
needs. Library supplies consist of accession sheets, book cards
and pockets, date-due slips, printed catalog cards from the H. W.
Wilson Company or the Library of Congress, plain catalog cards
to be typed for books for which printed cards are not available,
materials for lettering and shellacking books, stamps and stamp
pads, notices of various kinds, materials for mounting and circulating pictures and vertical file material, and similar things
needed to keep school library services going. Generally speaking,
it is better to order some supplies each year than to order a large
number of supplies in any year, even though there is some advantage in lower rates for quantity orders. Of course, printed
catalog cards must be ordered when orders are sent for corresponding books and cannot be bought in quantity.

Supplies for mending should be purchased from that part of
the school library funds set aside for mending and binding. (Types
of mending supplies are listed in Chapter 5.) The routine for
keeping library supplies on hand, suggested in the preceding
paragraph, applies equally to mending supplies. The purchase
of a small quantity out of each annual budget will assure a steady
supply of mending materials.

The amount of the annual budget needed for binding depends
entirely on how much must be done. If, for instance, little or no
binding has been done for several years, and a number of books
need to be rebound, it follows that a larger proportion of funds
will need to be allotted. For that reason, it is advisable to rebind books regularly rather than let them pile up for occasional
shipments to the bindery. While school libraries are not advised
to bind many magazines, it goes without saying that the allottment
for binding would need to be higher to cover the cost of binding

any magazines. In elementary school libraries, a large part of the budget assigned to binding will be absorbed by the cost of prebound books, discussed in Chapter 1.

The Contingent Fund

A workable budget for the school library should have some funds that are not assigned to any particular item to take care of unusual demands during the school year. As a general rule, the school librarian is allowed to use for the library money collected from fines. This provides a natural contingent fund for materials and supplies not covered by the budget. It is particularly convenient for small purchases made locally, thus saving the bother and delay of ordering. Records, of course, should be kept to indicate how all such funds are expended. On the other hand, in schools which do not allow fines to be kept and spent in the library, it will be essential to have a small contingent fund in the library budget itself.

A school library budget is illustrated, not as a model, but merely as an example of how a budget might be set up (Figure 44). This budget would be fairly typical of a high school which includes mostly standard subjects in its curriculum and where many of the students are preparing for college.

Records of School Library Finances

The first records of school library finances will undoubtedly be connected with book orders. In Chapter 1 it was suggested that, when the invoice has been received from the book dealer, the abbreviated name of the department or the area of instruction to which each book is to be charged should be entered from the order card beside the price paid for each item on the invoice. The total to be charged to each department is then entered at the lower left of the invoice for use in making the financial record discussed below. This notation on the invoice is shown in Figure 6.

The name A. B. C. School for Boys used in several of the examples was supplied by the Baker and Taylor Company who furnished an invoice based on the sample order shown in Figure 4.

Budget for the year, 1957-58

A.B.C. School for Boys

Total appropriation: 750.00

Budget for books:

Reference (15% of total)	112.50

Department allotments: 390.00

History, including travel	75.00
English, including literature	75.00
Social sciences	50.00
Science, including useful arts	75.00
Fine arts	40.00
Recreational material, including fiction and biography	75.00

Budget for non-book materials: 100.00

Magazines and newspapers (10% of total)	75.00
Vertical file material	10.00
Picture collection	5.00
Audio-visual (rental of films or film-strips)	15.00
Budget for supplies	20.00
Budget for mending and binding	75.00
Contingent fund	47.50
Total	750.00

FIGURE 44

Sample budget for school library

Actually the titles in the sample order were selected as examples of various types of entries rather than with a particular school library collection in mind. For the purpose of demonstration, however, it is assumed that the order was submitted by a high school library which also purchases some books on the elementary level, for which there exists a separate appropriation. Consideration in the financial records will be given only to books on the high school level in line with the sample budget.

If this routine is followed, the school librarian will have a financial record book with a page for the general budget and a separate page for each department, area of instruction, or Dewey Decimal Classification, according to the manner in which the book budget is set up. There will also be a page in the financial record book for other funds designated in the budget, such as supplies, mending and binding, etc. The sample budget (Figure 44) is, as will be noted, set up by departments. The financial record also follows this plan.

Before each invoice is submitted to the administration office for payment, the librarian will enter amounts to be charged to each account in the financial record. If the school library has not adopted a budget or is otherwise charging everything against the general fund, then only one record will be necessary (Figure 45). If, however, there is a budget as illustrated by Figure 44, then an additional record will be kept for each separate account, as suggested in the above paragraph. The example of a separate account illustrated is for the history department (Figure 46). Keeping these simple records will enable the school librarian at any time to know and be able to inform the various departments how much of the budget has been spent and how much still remains.

Records of Funds from Fines

In Chapter 3 a simple method was suggested for keeping account of the amount of fines taken in each day. (Figure 34.) A total from the daily slip should be transferred to a permanent record in the financial record book (Figure 47). A report of the

Financial Record: A.B.C. School for Boys (H.S.), 1957-58   750.00

Date of invoice	Number of order	Dealer from whom ordered	Amount of bill	Spent to date	Balance on hand
Sept. 2, 1957	1	Baker & Taylor	$35.68	$35.68	$714.32
Sept. 26, 1957	2	Macmillan	6.00	41.68	708.32
Oct. 9, 1957	3	McClurg	28.12	69.80	680.20
Oct. 27, 1957	4	Campbell & Hall	14.00	83.80	666.20
Nov. 6, 1957	5	Baker & Taylor	32.00	115.80	634.20

FIGURE 45

General financial record

Financial Record: History Department, 1957-58

$75.00

Date of invoice	Number of order	Dealer from whom ordered	Amount of bill	Spent to date	Balance on hand
Sept. 2, 1957	1	Baker & Taylor	$11.28	11.28	63.72
Oct. 9, 1957	3	McClurg	13.59	24.87	50.13
Nov. 6, 1957	5	Baker & Taylor	20.80	45.67	29.33

FIGURE 46

Departmental financial record

Record of fines collected - 1957-58.

Date	Sept.	Oct.	Nov.	Dec.	Jan.	Feb.	Mar.	Apr.	May	June
1										
2										
3										
4										
5										
6										
7										
8										
9										
10										
11										
12										
13										
14										
15										
16										
17										
18										
19										
20										
21										
22										
23										
24										
25										
26										
27										
28										
29										
30										
31										
Total										

Total for year _____

See other side for record of expenditures from fines

FIGURE 47

Record of fines collected

total amount of fines collected each month and at the end of the school year may be obtained from this completed record. If money from fines must be turned in to general school funds, rather than expended by the library, the above-mentioned record will be sufficient for the librarian to keep. It is suggested, however, that money collected in fines be deposited frequently in the administrative office for safe-keeping, regardless of how it is to be spent.

In case the librarian does spend fine money for needed items, a record should be kept of all expenditures. This simple record may be kept on the back of the permanent fine record for the year or on an additional sheet.

Information from financial records may be incorporated in periodic reports to the school principal and should certainly be made a part of the annual report to the administration, as discussed in Chapter 7.

Conclusion

The school library is supported by an annual appropriation, usually on a per pupil basis, as required by the standards under which the library operates. The school librarian is advised to set up a budget for spending money from the appropriation, after consultation with teachers and administrators. Simple records, regularly kept, both of money appropriated for the school library and funds accruing from fines, will enable the school librarian at any time to give an account of what money has been expended and what still remains. The wise expenditure of all money appropriated to the school library will prove a good recommendation when it becomes necessary to ask for an increase in the appropriation to provide better library services.

CHAPTER 7

SCHOOL LIBRARY REPORTS

Introduction

One of the best methods for keeping the school administration informed about what takes place in the library is the report which the librarian prepares and submits. Those interested in library reports are the school principal, the superintendent of the school system, the local supervisor of school libraries (or the general supervisor of the system if there is no school library supervisor), and the state department of education, particularly the state supervisor of school libraries. A report on the school library is usually included in the annual report required by the state department of education of each individual school. Wherever a school is accredited by the regional association of its area, an annual report, including one on the school library, must also be submitted to that accrediting body. Both the report for the state department of education and the regional association are in printed form and should be filled out by the school librarian or from information furnished by him.

The nature and frequency of reports on the local level are determined by a plan established by the local administration in cooperation with the librarian. Unfortunately, many school libraries submit no reports except the printed forms mentioned above and, in a great many other schools, reports are handled in a haphazard manner. When going into a new position, the librarian should follow the plan for submitting reports to the local administration already in effect. In a school where library reports have not previously been customary, the school librarian will do well to initiate the regular routine of preparing and submitting reports to the administration.

Materials for the Library Report

Materials for school library reports exist in great abundance if records have been consistently kept as suggested in preceding chapters. Statistics on various phases of school library work may be incorporated with telling effect into reports. These fall into the following categories:

1. The number of pupils using the library.

Wherever there is scheduled attendance, as is the rule in most elementary schools and many junior high schools, the pupils come by classes and so their number can easily be determined. In the case of high schools which hold study halls in the library, the librarian may have to estimate the percentage of pupils using library materials, since many may be studying text-books or performing other duties not involving library use. Where attendance is voluntary, with free passage between study hall and library, a surprisingly large number of pupils may use even a small library during a given period. Suggestions were made in Chapter 4 for keeping a sampling of library attendance. In addition, there are often groups of pupils from various classrooms who come to use the library. While the exact number of pupils using the library is not an especially important factor, it is significant in indicating the librarian's work load. A report of library use is one method of making the administration aware of demands on the library and the work of the librarian in meeting them.

2. The size of the collection of materials.

At the end of each school year, records will show how many books and other materials have been added, how many lost or discarded, and how many still remain in the collection (Figure 39). This record of books should be kept by divisions of the Dewey Decimal Classification since that is the form in which the information is usually requested. Magazine records will indicate the number of magazines for which the library subscribes and whether any are received as gifts. There will also be a record of the back issues which are kept for reference use and the length of time they are kept. While very accurate records might consume more time than is justified, the librarian should be able to estimate the approximate amount of materials in the vertical file and picture collection. There will also be a record of audio-visual materials belonging to the school library and those available from other sources. Though statistics on materials do not necessarily indicate adequacy of the library collection, they do suggest what the library has to offer.

3. The amount of materials circulated.

The types and amount of materials circulated from the school library indicate one phase of the school library's total service. Following routines suggested in Chapter 3, there should be full and accurate records of books, magazines, pictures, material from the vertical file and audio-visual materials borrowed from the library. Records are kept daily, then entered in a monthly record from which totals for the school year may be obtained, as described in Chapter 3. Not only the statistics themselves but comparisons with statistics of past years may well be included in reports.

4. The reference questions handled in the library.

The number of questions brought to the reference desk of the school library is indicative of the amount of reference work done by various classes of the school. The questions also show what keeps the librarian busy for the major part of the school day.

Even more important than the actual number of questions, however, is information as to the types of questions asked and how successfully they have been answered. Failure to answer certain questions may point up what reference materials are not available in the library collection and lead to the purchase of additional materials. Unanswered questions may also have some significance in evaluating the quality of reference service in the school library.

5. Special services of the library.

This part of the report will be concerned with such services as the collections loaned for use in classrooms and the materials handled as classroom reserves in the library. Some indication as to the circulation of reserves during the day and for overnight use will also prove pertinent. An occasional account of books requested for personal reserve may also be used in reports.

Group meetings in the library, apart from those concerned with regular attendance, may be reported. Activities of the school librarian in visiting classrooms or teaching the use of the library are likewise of interest for reports.

6. School library publicity.

Included here will be information as to special book displays in the library and elsewhere in the school, programs arranged by the library for assembly or at the time of outstanding events, such as Book Week, book reviews or book talks by the librarian or members of the library club, and library items reported through the medium of the school publication or weekly newspaper. Displays arranged in the library through the cooperation of various classes, often in connection with some current project, should also be included in reports.

7. School library finances.

Records of school library finances should always be included in library reports. The appropriation for the library, the budget and expenditures, fines collected and expended are all a part of the financial picture. There should also be a report of any money from sources other than the regular appropriation, such as gifts from the Parent-Teacher Association or other organizations.

Frequency of School Library Reports

Frequency of reports will depend largely on the local situation. In some schools the librarian submits a brief report at the end of each school month or six-weeks period, when teachers submit grades and reports are prepared for pupils. Under this plan the library report is presented at a regular, stated time and the administration will be systematically informed about the library. Less frequent reports would be adequate in many situations. Periodic reports furnish material for the annual report and lighten the task of preparing it. Every school library should submit an annual report, a fairly comprehensive summary of library activities for the school year.

Form of Reports

Much reporting of school library activities will be done orally in conferences between the librarian and the principal. It is well for the record if the librarian can incorporate much of what is said in conferences into the written report.

Periodic written reports should be presented as briefly as is consistent with efficiency. A one-page report is often read when one more lengthy might be laid aside and buried under mounting papers. Some pictorial form that tells facts and figures at a glance is often practical. Fortunate is the school librarian who can, or finds an assistant who can, produce really clever stick figures, charts or graphs and other pictorial representations of statistics or other information that otherwise might prove dull.

The annual report, intended as a permanent part of the school records, should be more comprehensive and should be typed in good form. The report will need to be duplicated in sufficient quantity so that copies may be sent to interested persons in the administration suggested earlier in the chapter. It is also advisable to make the annual report available to teachers in the school. A copy, of course, will be kept in the library as part of the complete record of library activities.

The report itself will probably be a combination of narrative and statistics, with comments on the statistics. Frequent headings and sub-heads help to break up the page and make it easier to read the report and to locate specific sections.

In addition to furnishing a summary of the activities of "the school library at work," the annual report should also point up the library's needs. This part of the report will probably include requests for a larger appropriation, particularly if the library is not yet meeting standards set by the state department or regional accrediting association, additional help for the librarian (professional, clerical, or pupil assistants) and provision for more space to house materials or to furnish better service to teachers and pupils. The current need may well be an additional section of the card catalog or vertical file, a book truck, or more shelving, none of which would be provided by the library budget, which is only for materials and supplies. If the school library is expanding holdings in audio-visual materials, there would obviously be a need for additional funds to purchase audio-visual materials and for additional staff to administer their use.

Purposes of the Library Reports

The purposes to be served by library reports seem fairly obvious. They are the best means of keeping the administration regularly informed about service to the school through its library. Reports are useful in pointing out to the library staff and the administration how nearly the library is meeting its objectives, which are the library's strong features and where the weak points are. Reports furnish the most complete record of library work, year after year, and offer a basis for comparison in various phases of work. Because statistics are needed for reports, there is a greater incentive for keeping records that are complete and accurate. Often reports may be used to justify to taxpayers the expenditures for school library service, still considered in some quarters as an educational frill.

Conclusion

Reports are a definite part of school library work and should be prepared and submitted according to a regular plan adequate for the local situation. They should be submitted to the school administrators of the system, as well as to the state department of education and the regional accrediting associations. Material for reports is gathered from records of work in various departments, such as acquisitions, preparation for use, circulation of various types of materials, service to teachers and pupils, and maintenance of the library collection. Reports serve as a device to measure the adequacy of library service to the school.

APPENDIX

AIDS FOR THE SELECTION OF MATERIALS FOR SCHOOL LIBRARIES *

GENERAL AIDS

Adventuring with Books; a Reading List for the Elementary Grades. Chicago, National Council of Teachers of English, c1956. 146p. 75c

A Basic Book Collection for Elementary Grades. 6th ed. Chicago, American Library Association, 1956. 133p. $2.00

A Basic Book Collection for Junior High Schools. 2d ed. Chicago, American Library Association, 1956. 127p. $2.00

A Basic Book Collection for High Schools. 6th ed. Chicago, American Library Association, 1957. 186p. $2.75

Book Bait; Detailed Notes on Adult Books Popular with Young People; comp. for the Association of Young People's Librarians by Elinor Walker. Chicago, American Library Association, 1957. 88p. $1.25

Books for Tired Eyes; a List of Books in Large Print; comp. by Charlotte Matson and Lela Larson. 4th ed. Chicago, American Library Association, 1951. Juvenile Books, p. 60-75. $1.00

⅄ *Books for You; a List for Leisure Reading for Use by Students in Senior High Schools.* Chicago, National Council of Teachers of English, c1951. 130p. 40c

Children's Catalog. 9th ed. rev. New York, H. W. Wilson Company, 1956. 852p. Sold on the service basis. (Kept up to date by supplements)

Patterns in Reading; an Annotated Book List for Young People, by Jean Carolyn Roos. Chicago, American Library Association, 1954. 138p. $2.00

Standard Catalog for High School Libraries. 7th ed. rev. New York, H. W. Wilson Company, 1957. 948p. Sold on the service basis. (Kept up to date by supplements)

Treasure for the Taking; a Book List for Boys and Girls, by Anne Thaxter Eaton. Rev. ed. New York, Viking Press, c1957. 322p. $3.50

⅄ *Your Reading; a List for Junior High Schools.* Chicago, National Council of Teachers of English, c1954. 126p. 60c

* The prices given are correct as of the time of publication. Because of the frequency of price changes, the reader is advised to use them only as estimates.

AIDS FOR SELECTION OF MATERIALS ON SPECIAL SUBJECTS

Books about Negro Life for Children; comp. by Augusta Braxston Baker. New York, New York Public Library, 1957. 24p. 25c

Books to Help Build International Understanding. Rev. June 1954 together with a supplement of radio recordings selected for children and young people; comp. by Nora E. Beust and Gertrude G. Broderick. Washington, D.C. U.S. Dept. of Health, Education and Welfare. 37p. Mimeographed. Gratis.

✴ *Reading Ladders for Human Relations.* Rev. and enl. ed., 1954, by Margaret M. Heaton and Helen B. Lewis. Washington, D.C. American Council on Education, ₁1955₁ 215p. $1.25

Vocations in Fact and Fiction; a Selective, Annotated List of Books for Career Backgrounds and Inspirational Reading; comp. by Kathryn A. Haebich. Chicago, American Library Association, 1953. 62p. 50c

We Build Together; a Reader's Guide to Negro Life and Literature for Elementary and High School Use; comp. by Charlemae Rollins. Rev. ed. Chicago, National Council of Teachers of English, c1948. 71p. 25c

SUBJECT INDEXES TO MATERIALS

Subject and Title Index to Short Stories for Children. Chicago, American Library Association, 1955. 333p. $4.50

Subject Index to Books for Intermediate Grades, by Eloise Rue. 2d ed. Chicago, American Library Association, 1950. 493p. $6.00

Subject Index to Books for Primary Grades, by Eloise Rue. Chicago, American Library Association, 1943. 236p. $2.50
——. First Supplement. 1946. 197p. $1.25

Subject Index to Poetry for Children and Young People; comp. by Violet Sells and others. Chicago, American Library Association, 1957. 582p. $9.00

AIDS FOR SELECTION OF MATERIALS FOR SLOW READERS

Fare for the Reluctant Reader; comp. for Capital Area School Development Association by Anita E. Dunn and others. Rev. ed. Albany, N.Y., New York State College for Teachers, c1952. 167p. $1.25

Gateways to Readable Books; an Annotated Graded List of Books in Many Fields, for Adolescents Who Find Reading Difficult, by Ruth Strang and others. 3d ed. New York, H. W. Wilson Company, 1958. 181p. $3.00

Good Books for Poor Readers; comp. by George Spache. Gainesville, Fla., The University of Florida, 1954. 114p. $1.50

High Interest Low Vocabulary Booklist; comp. by Donald D. Durrell and Helen Blair Sullivan. Boston, Boston University School of Education, c1952. 35p. 75c

AIDS FOR THE SELECTION OF INEXPENSIVE MATERIALS

Free and Inexpensive Learning Materials. 7th ed. Nashville, Tenn. Division of Surveys and Field Services, George Peabody College for Teachers, 1956. 244p. $1.00

Inexpensive Books for Boys and Girls; comp. by the Subcommittee on Inexpensive Books for Boys and Girls of the A.L.A. Editorial Committee. 3d ed. rev. Chicago, American Library Association, 1952. 25p. 75c

Sources of Free and Inexpensive Educational Materials. Chicago, Field Enterprises, 1955. 192p. $5.00

AIDS FOR THE SELECTION OF PAMPHLETS, PERIODICALS AND VISUAL MATERIALS

Educational Film Guide. 11th ed., 1953 and 1954-1958 revised supplement. New York, H. W. Wilson Company, 1953 and 1958. 1037p.; 448p. Prices quoted on request.

Filmstrip Guide. 3d ed., 1954, and 1955-1958 revised supplement. New York, H. W. Wilson Company, 1954 and 1959. 410p.; about 250p. Prices quoted on request.

Pamphlets for Children's Library Collections, prepared by Isabella Jinnette. Baltimore, Md., Enoch Pratt Free Library, 1953. 19p. (Mimeographed) 15c

Vertical File Index. New York, H. W. Wilson Company, 1932—Monthly. $6.00 per year.

NOTE: For aid in the selection of magazines, consult list at the end of the *Basic Book Collection* for each level of school libraries.

CURRENT BOOK REVIEWING PERIODICALS

The Booklist and Subscription Books Bulletin; a Guide to Current Books. Published semi-monthly, September-July, and once only in August, by the American Library Association. $6.00. Sections: Children's Books, Books for Young People, and Subscription Books Bulletin.

Bulletin of the Center for Children's Books. Published monthly except August by the University of Chicago Press for the University of Chicago, Graduate Library School. $4.50

The Horn Book. Published six times a year by the Horn Book, Inc. $4.50

Library Journal. Published twice a month, September-June, monthly in July and August by R. R. Bowker Company. $9.00. *Junior Libraries.* Published monthly as part of *Library Journal* but paged separately and obtainable as a separate. $2.50

New York Herald Tribune Book Review. Published weekly by the New York Herald Tribune. $2.50 Section: For Boys and Girls.

The New York Times Book Review. Published weekly by The New York Times Company. $4.80 Section: New Books for Younger Readers' Library (title varies)

The Saturday Review. Published weekly by Saturday Review, Inc. $7.00. Section: Books for Young People (one issue each month)

Wilson Library Bulletin. Published monthly, except July and August, by the H. W. Wilson Company. $3.00 Section: Current Reference Books.

MANUALS FOR TEACHING
THE USE OF THE LIBRARY *

Aldrich, Ella Virginia. *Using Books and Libraries.* 3d ed. New York, Prentice-Hall, 1951. 102p. $1.25.

Berner, Elsa R. *Integrating Library Instruction with Classroom Teaching at Plainview Junior High School.* Chicago, American Library Association, 1958. 110p. $2.75.

Boyd, Jessie Edna and others. *Books, Libraries and You; a Handbook on the Use of Reference Books and the Reference Sources of the Library.* New ed. New York, Scribner, 1949. 143p. $2.32.

Cook, Margaret Gerry. *New Library Key.* New York, H. W. Wilson Company, 1956. 136p. $1.00.

Ingles, May and McCague, Anna. *Teaching the Use of Books and Libraries; a Manual for Teachers and Librarians.* 4th ed. rev. New York, H. W. Wilson Company, 1944. 204p. $1.80 (out of print but still useful where libraries have a copy)

Mott, Carolyn and Baisden, Leo B. *Children's Book on How To Use Books and Libraries.* New York, Scribner, 1955. 207p. $2.44.

Rossoff, Martin. *Using Your High School Library.* New York, H. W. Wilson Company, 1952. 75p. 70c

Scripture, Elizabeth and Greer, Margaret R. *Find it Yourself! A Brief Course in the Use of Books and Libraries.* 4th ed. rev. New York, H. W. Wilson Company, 1955. 64p. 40c

Toser, Marie Antoinette. *Library Manual: A Study-Work Manual of Lessons on the Use of Books and Libraries.* 5th ed. New York, H. W. Wilson Company, 1955. 94p. 70c

* The prices given are correct as of the time of publication. Because of the frequency of price changes, the reader is advised to use them only as estimates.

DIRECTORY OF PUBLISHERS
AND SUPPLIERS

This is a directory only of firms which publish books or handle supplies mentioned in this work. There are of course many others. A much fuller list is to be found in the Bowker Company's annual *Literary Market Place* with sub-title "the business directory of American book publishing" which includes lists of publishers, book manufacturers and binders, wholesalers, prebinders, remainder dealers and many others. While school libraries would probably not have this publication, it should be available for consultation in many public and college libraries. The July-August 1958 issue of the *A.L.A. Bulletin* carries an extensive "Guide to Library Equipment and Supplies" which should also prove useful.

American Library Association. 50 East Huron St. Chicago 11
American News Company. 131 Varick St. New York 13
    (Branches in many of the larger cities)
Baker and Taylor Company. 1405 North Broad St. Hillside, N.J.
Boston University School of Education. 332 Bay State Road. Boston 15
R. R. Bowker Company. 62 West 45th St. New York 36
Bro-Dart Industries. 90 East Alpine St. Newark 5, N.J. and 1888 South
    Sepulveda Blvd. Los Angeles 25
Burgess Publishing Company. 426-428 6th St. Minneapolis 15, Minn.
Demco Library Supplies, Inc. Madison, Wis. and New Haven 2, Conn.
E. P. Dutton and Company, Inc. 300 4th Ave. New York 10
Enoch Pratt Free Library. Cathedral and Mulberry Sts. Baltimore 1, Md.
Farrar, Straus and Cudahy, Inc. 101 5th Ave. New York 3
F. W. Faxon Company. 83-91 Francis St.   Back Bay, Boston 15
Fideler Company. Grand Rapids 2, Mich.
Field Enterprises, Inc. Merchandise Mart Plaza. Chicago 54
Follett Library Book Company. 1018 West Washington Blvd. Chicago 7

Forest Press, Inc. Lake Placid Club. Essex County, N.Y.

The Frontier Press Company. Lafayette Bldg. Buffalo 3, N.Y.

Gaylord Brothers, Inc. Syracuse 4, N.Y. and Stockton, Calif.

George Peabody College for Teachers. Survey and Field Services. 2000
    21st Ave. S. Nashville 4, Tenn.

E. M. Hale and Company. 320 South Barstow St. Eau Claire, Wis.

Harper and Brothers. 49 East 33rd St. New York 16

Horn Book, Inc. 585 Boyleston St. Boston 15

H. R. Huntting Company, Inc. Springfield 3, Mass.

Junior Literary Guild. Garden City, N.Y.

Keystone View Company. Meadville, Pa.

Alfred A. Knopf, Inc. 501 Madison Ave. New York 22

Library Bureau, Remington Rand. 315 Fourth Ave. New York 10
(Branches in many of the larger cities)

Library Journal. 62 West 45th St. New York 56

A. C. McClurg and Company. 333 East Ontario St. Chicago 11

Marador Corporation. 1722 Glendale Blvd. Los Angeles 26

Mayfair Agency. 40 North Van Brunt St. Englewood, N.J.

National Council of Teachers of English. 211 West 68th St. Chicago 21

National Education Association of the United States. 1201 16th St. N.W.
Washington, D.C.

New York Herald Tribune, Inc. 230 West 41st St. New York 36

The New York Times Company. Times Square, New York 36

New York World-Telegram and Sun. 125 Barclay St. New York 15

Don R. Phillips, Inc. P. O. Box 57. Vandalia, Mich.

Saturday Review, Inc. 25 West 45th St. New York 36

Scott, Foresman and Company. 433 E. Erie St. Chicago 11

U. S. Government Printing Office. Washington 25, D.C.

U. S. Library of Congress. Washington 25, D.C.

University of Chicago Press. 5750 Ellis Ave. Chicago 37

H. W. Wilson Company. 950-972 University Ave. New York 52

GLOSSARY OF LIBRARY TERMS

Accession Book

A loose-leaf book in which all volumes are entered as they are received in the library. See also Accession Number.

Accession Number

A number assigned to each volume as it is received in the library. It is taken from the line on which the volume is accessioned in the accession book. The accession number is the one thing which distinguishes one book from every other book in the library.

Agent

One who represents a publisher or dealer in the sale of books and other materials.

Analytic Card

A card in the card catalog which refers to only part of a book. It may be an author, subject or title analytic depending on the type of material to which it refers.

Annotation

A brief statement giving information about a book. Annotations are found in book selection aids and other bibliographies and are designed to tell "who, when, where, what and why."

Back strip

A strip of book cloth or similar material which covers the spine of the book. Term used in mending or binding to identify material connecting back and front boards or sides.

Backing Material. See Super

Bibliography

A list of books and other materials on a given subject or by a certain author.

Bindery

A firm which binds books and periodicals for library use.

Book End

A support of metal or wood to hold upright a group of books on the shelf.

Book Jacket

The colorful paper cover which comes around most new books. Also called Dust Jacket.

Buckram

A heavy type of book cloth used in prebinding or rebinding books.

Business Entry. See Trade Entry.

Call Number

The number on the spine of the book and on the catalog cards, by which the book is called for. It is composed of a Dewey Decimal Classification number and a number which refers to the particular book.

Card Catalog

An alphabetical file of cards which serves as an index to books on the shelves. Each card carries the call number of a book—the same call number that is lettered on the book's spine.

Catalog Card

Any card in the card catalog. The card may be an author, title or subject card depending on what is on the first line of the card.

Certified Bindery

A bindery that has been certified by the Library Binders Institute as complying with standards set up for binding.

Charge

As a noun: A record of the loan of a book. As a verb: To record a loan.

Charging Tray

A rectangular box used to hold book cards of books that have been charged out in circulation.

Collate

To examine material being prepared for use to make sure there are no defects. This is done when books are received on order or being sent to or received from the bindery.

Consideration File

A file of materials which seem desirable for purchase. Also called Want File.

Dealer

One who deals in books and other materials purchased by libraries. Also referred to as jobber.

Dewey Decimal Classification

A system of classification used in most libraries and devised by Melvil Dewey. It divides all knowledge into ten main classes which in turn are divided by tens to provide numbers for a wide variety of subjects.

Discharge

The opposite of charge. The process of returning to the collection a book which has been loaned.

Double-Stitched Binding

Two pieces of cloth stitched together in two rows of varying distances apart to fit over the spine of books of all thicknesses. Useful as an easily manipulated super in recasing books. Obtainable in rolls from library supply houses.

Dust Jacket. See Book Jacket

End Papers

The leaves used by a binder at the front and back of the book. One side of the end paper is pasted to the inside cover. Also called End Leaves, Lining Papers, End Sheets.

Hinge

The part of the book identified by the groove along the front and back covers where they join the backstrip, allowing the book to be opened easily.

Information File. See Vertical File

Key Page. See Secret Page

Margin Papers

Strips of paper of the color and texture of book pages. Used in mending.

Open Shelves

Shelves, usually around the walls in school libraries, to which the readers have easy access.

Ownership Mark

The name of the library stamped on books and other materials to identify them.

Prebinding

The process of resewing books and placing them in durable covers before they are purchased.

Reading Shelves

The process of reading the call numbers of books on the shelves to determine their proper position.

Rebinding

The process of resewing and putting books into durable covers after they have become worn.

Reference Books

Books containing general information which are kept in a special collection in the library.

Reserves, Class

Books and other materials requested by a teacher who wishes them kept in the library for use by students. Such materials circulate only for overnight use. Also known as Teacher Reserves.

Reserves, Personal

Books reserved for use by readers on individual requests. Also known as Reader Reserves.

Secret Page

A page chosen by each library on which are entered the trade entry, accession number, and name of the library as a means of identification. Also known as Key Page.

Shelf List

An index of cards, one for each title owned by the library, arranged by call number as the books stand on the shelves. Useful in keeping record of all books and in taking inventory.

Snag

A book for which no card can be found in circulation records.

Spine

The part of the book's cover that faces the reader as the book stands on the shelf. Usually there is printed on the spine the author, title and publisher. The call number is added when the book becomes part of a library collection.

Super

A piece of coarse cloth glued across the signatures forming the body of the book and reinforcing the back, enabling end papers to be pasted to the book cover.

Title-Page

The page near the front of the book on which is given the author, title, edition, if other than the first, publisher with the place of publication and date, and the series if the book belongs to one.

Trade Entry

The record of the source, price and date of acquisition placed in each book as it is being prepared for use. Also known as Business Entry.

Vertical File

A file of clippings, pamphlets and other material to supplement the book collection, especially in current events, local history, etc. Also known as Information File.

Want File. See Consideration File.

INDEX

(Figures in italics indicate pages upon which illustrations occur.)